YIPPEE KI-YAY
MOTHERF*CKER
A TRIVIA GUIDE TO DIE-HARD

MARK LESLIE

Stark Publishing

Stark Entertainment
An Imprint of Stark Publishing
Waterloo, Ontario
www.starkpublishing.ca

Publisher's Note: This work is intended as a celebration
of a modern classic film that the author adores, and of
all the people involved in its production. It was
compiled with the intention of offering fans of the *Die
Hard* movie franchise a concise collection of various
trivia and insights as gathered from numerous sources.

Yippee Ki-Yay Motherf*cker / Mark Leslie
July 2023

Hardcover ISBN: 978-1-989351-88-8
Paperback ISBN: 978-1-989351-87-1
eBook ISBN: 978-1-989351-86-4

DEDICATION

For my son,
Alexander

And for every single person involved in any way in the making of Die Hard. *Your work entertained me, my son, and millions of other movie fans in these past 35 years.*

TABLE OF CONTENTS

"Welcome to the Party, Pal!"

Bruce Willis, "Die Hard" (1988) 20th Century Fox /
File Reference # 34082-132THA

WELCOME TO THE PARTY, PAL!

Foreword by Sweary Historian James Fell

The late '80s was a boon for Beretta sales. Specifically, the 92F model.

The 9mm pistol with its 15-round magazine received a major product placement in *Lethal Weapon*, with Danny Glover doing the kind of firearm dirty talk that makes ammosexuals touch themselves. "Fifteen in the mag, one up the pipe, wide ejection port, no feed jams." *Ooohhhh dammit now I need to change my underwear.*

A year later all those *not* members of well-regulated militias recognized Martin Riggs's shooty boom toy in the hands of another doesn't-play-by-the-rules copaganda hero: John McClane. It wasn't just the Italian-made Beretta 92F (a company that's been in business for half a millennium) Detective John Boy was using to send Eurotrash terrorists off to the great certainty, but the *exact same* prop gun that Mel Gibson caressed while turning paper targets into smiley faces. I wonder how the notoriously antisemitic Mel would have felt if they gave him an Israeli-made Desert Eagle to shoot at fleeing helicopters with. Probably would have needed to do a bunch of Hail Marys afterward or some shit.

Anyfuckingway, let's talk terrorists. I mean thieves. Not common thieves, exceptional ones.

Hans *had* been a terrorist, a member of the "Volksfrei Movement," which never actually existed. None of the terrorist groups named are real, but they're all based on real organizations.

Volksfrei was intended to represent the *Baader-Meinhof-Gruppe*, also known as the Red Army Faction. They were a West German urban guerilla movement that bought into all that communism bullshit. Operating from 1970 to 1998, they killed a total of thirty-four people via bombings and targeted assassinations in their "anti-imperialistic struggle." I mean yeah western capitalism has a lot to answer for but embracing Soviet-style communism as the alternative was just a big bucket of dumb-fuck.

I guess Hans got tired of this idea that the state would own everything and said Karl Marx can inhale a big bag of dog farts because Gruber wanted to be owning his own shit and sitting on a beach earning twenty percent with his stolen bearer bonds. Twenty percent? The fuck kind of miracle worker is his portfolio manager?

My ADHD wants me to do a sidebar on the history of bearer bonds but it's kinda boring so google that shit if you want.

As part of Hans's ploy to steal an assload of cash he fakes out the cops by making them think he still embraces all that revolutionary freedom fighter stuff with the goal of getting the FBI involved because that electromagnetic seal has gotta come down. He gets on the radio with Assistant Deputy Dwayne T. Small Dick Energy Robinson and demands the release of his "comrades in arms around the world languishing in prison." The groups he names are the "Seven members of the New Provo Front" in Northern Ireland, the "Five imprisoned leaders of *Liberté de Quebec*," and the "nine members of the Asian Dawn movement" in Sri Lanka that he read about in *Time Magazine*.

As I said, none of those terrorist groups existed by those names. The New Provo front is based on the Provisional Irish Republican Army that sought to end British rule in Northern Ireland. Interestingly, the 9/11 attacks accelerated the IRA's decommissioning and embracing of the peace process because seeing videos of planes flying into buildings soured much of the world on any form of terrorism.

Liberté de Québec was based on the *Front de libération du Québec* (FLQ), a terrorist group fighting for Quebec to separate from the rest of Canada. In 1970 the group kidnapped the deputy premier of Quebec Pierre LaPorte then later executed him. Within a dozen years all involved were walking free, so there weren't any imprisoned FLQ leaders when *Die Hard* came out in 1988. In fact, the killing of

LaPorte and the arrests that followed embittered many on the organization and it rapidly fell into decline.

And Asian Dawn was of course meant to represent the Liberation Tigers of Tamil Eelam (LTTE), a militant separatist group questing for an independent home for Hindu Tamils in northeast Sri Lanka. They were by far the most vicious and deadly of the three groups, with the quarter-century-long civil war between the LTTE and the Sri Lankan government resulting in 100,000 deaths, close to half of them civilians.

While Hans gives his spiel our hero John is listening in and says, "What the fuck?" like he rightly believes this is all bullshit, but it's important to note that terrorists taking hostages as a ploy to gain freedom for their "comrades in arms" has been a common occurrence. As an example, prior to murdering eleven Israeli athletes and coaches in Munich in 1972, the Black September group demanded the release of 234 mostly Palestinians held in Israeli prisons. Israel said get fucked and the Germans fucked up the rescue and a lotta people died and then the Germans fucked up again a month later. The following October 29, Palestinian terrorists hijacked Lufthansa Flight 615 and said hey you need to free the three surviving Black September terrorists who killed those Israelis or we're gonna kill everyone on this plane and the West German government said yeah sure okay and let the terrorists go because Germany has something of a history of not giving a fuck about Jewish lives.

In conclusion, *Die Hard* is definitely copaganda but also good fun so as long as you realize that there is a serious problem with the militarization and infiltration of white supremacy of policing in America. Sorry to be a downer on that front. Go ahead and enjoy the movie.

And also, enjoy the shit out of this book.

—James Fell, author of
On This Day in History Sh!t Went Down

WHY WRITE THIS BOOK?
WHY RELEASE IT NOW?
AND WHY THIS AUTHOR?

A Die-Hard fan's Introduction

*D*ie *Hard* is one of those rare films that is not only well known but also beloved by so many people. It's also a movie that is often watched and re-watched numerous times by those who love it.

I'm one of those people.

I can't remember the details associated with my first viewing of the film—I suspect it was a VHS rental—but it's definitely a movie I have already watched too many times to count.

Watching *Die Hard* around Christmas time has become an annual ritual for me. And, ever since my son, who is just turning nineteen around the time this book is being released, reached a somewhat appropriate age, it's a film we have regularly enjoyed together during the holidays.

Like so many people, I have made watching *Die Hard* on an annual basis a regular and repeating ritual. Considering the millions of movies available for people to do that with, this film holds a unique place alongside perhaps a hundred or so more films that are regularly re-watched.

While you can find *Die Hard* listed on various "most rewatched" or "most re-watchable" films, it's notable that a June 2020 study from Now TV, a streaming service in the UK, revealed that *Die Hard*, along with *Dirty Dancing* and *The Wizard of Oz* topped the list of the most re-watched movies of all time, with the average UK adult having seen those movies 12 times each.

Simply, *Die Hard* is a film that stands out in numerous ways. Not just as a block-buster movie, but as one that raised the bar for action films and created a franchise that fans have itched to return to again and again.

In addition to four movie sequels, graphic novels, and video games, *Die*

Hard has inspired several non-fiction books that take a look at the film we love.

The book *Die Hard: The Ultimate Visual History* by James Mottram and David S. Cohen is a 240-page massive coffee-table book that is heavy enough that John McClane could likely use as a makeshift bludgeoning weapon to take down at least a few bad guys. Not only is the book filled with insightful stories about the five films in the franchise, but the photos, art-work, special inserts and pop-out bonus art and items make it a multi-dimensional experience for any die-hard fan.

Why We Love Die Hard by Kim Taylor-Foster was released in September of 2022 by Running Press. This book is a gorgeous hardcover with spectacular art and design by Ink Bad Company (the creative studio and alter ego of JC Guerrero). Taylor-Foster does a most amazing job of explor-ing so much of what makes the film one that so many people adore.

If you haven't read these books, I strongly suggest you check them out. Among the dozens of articles and videos used to research this book, I returned to these two sources numerous times in my own research. They are two I would highly recommend, both for content as well as for the spectacular visual presentation they each offer in their unique ways.

So, with such great books about the movie already available, why would I bother to write this one?

That's a great question.

And it's one I asked myself numerous times in the past couple of years.

The answer is, at once, both simple and dynamically layered.

Part of me wants to say something like:

Because it's there, motherfucker.

Perhaps I am driven, in the same manner that John McClane was compelled to take down the terrorists; because he was there, and so were they.

But it's more than that.

This movie, and the franchise itself, has inspired, entertained, and repeatedly thrilled me countless times since I first watched it.

I have reveled not only in sharing a first viewing of *Die Hard* with people and engaging in long conversations about it well after the final credits have finished rolling, but I've studied and read up on it, gathering bits of information that I'm eager to share back with the world in my own way.

As a book nerd, when I realized that *Die Hard* was based upon a then out-of-print Roderick Thorp novel called *Nothing Lasts Forever*, I hunted it down via used bookstores and have bought no fewer than a half dozen copies of it over the years. The reason for the constant re-purchasing was because I kept loaning it out to friends.

Of course, during the research for this book, I purchased a more expensive first edition hardcover of that original 1979 novel.

I also sought out *58 Minutes* the Walter Wager novel that the premise and main plot for *Die Hard 2: Die Harder* was adapted from.

It has long been important to me to better learn, better understand why I—and so many other people—are so drawn to the movie. Maybe it's because, as a writer,

I'm always curious to explore how to recreate something like that in my own fiction.

But also, as a writer who has researched and collected various eerie stories of ghostly hauntings and unexplained phenomena, it's in my nature to read, listen, seek out information, and then gather it together to share in a themed volume.

And, as a storyteller, I enjoy adding my own unique voice to that retelling.

It could also be related to the fact that July 2023 marks the 35th anniversary of the theatrical release of *Die Hard* and I couldn't let that pass without wanting to celebrate it in some way; by sharing a collection of trivia tidbits and other behind-the-scenes and interesting factoids about the movie.

Yes, much of what I share in this book you can find in various articles, books, special features on Blu-ray and DVD releases, and in online repositories.

But I've compiled them here, in my own way, as part of a pet project—creating the type of book that I, as a lover of the movie, would enjoy having and reading.

I did something similar with another film that I've watched and enjoyed countless times: *Planes, Trains and Automobiles*. In the fall of 2022, I released the book *The Canadian Mounted: A Trivia Guide to Planes, Trains and Automobiles*. The book's title, and design, was a nod to a book that Del Griffith (John Candy) is seen reading at LaGuardia airport near the beginning of the movie. It was mostly me pursuing a personal passion. I expected that perhaps a small handful of people might be intrigued by it, recognizing it from the film. But it turned into something people seemed to really love.

And I realized that a book written fueled by that type of love can be contagious.

So I thought I'd do it again with another film that I have seen countless times, and will continue to watch at least once a year.

Because, like John McClane's penchant for trouble, my love for this film, and all it brings, is something I just can't ignore.

Not only is it one of those movies that I talk about endlessly, but it has also incorporated itself into my own fiction. One of my main characters, Michael Andrews, from my "Canadian Werewolf" humorous urban fantasy series, is a fan of the movies, and even makes cheeky references to the *Die Hard* franchise and quotes John McClane.

My obsession seems, if you'll allow me the pun, to die hard.

Perhaps, because you've picked this up, you're very much like me.

In which case, in the way that Nakatomi Plaza looms forebodingly in the distance, that's a bit of a foreshadow of the ride we're both about to go on.

But, alas, your young chauffeur—on his first day of his new job—awaits to take you to that Christmas party you've arrived for. Don't worry if it's your first limo ride; I'm sure he'll be cool if you ride up front with him.

And I'm sure I don't need to remind you to fasten your seatbelt.

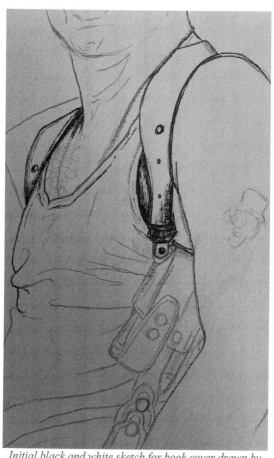

*Initial black and white sketch for book cover drawn by
Canadian artist Nikolette Jones*

www.nikolettejonesart.com

VIEW FROM THE 35TH FLOOR

A high-level look at the movie

On Christmas Eve 1988 NYPD Detective John McClane arrives in Los Angeles in the hopes of making amends with his estranged wife. Moments after catching up with Holly at a party held by her employer, the Nakatomi Corporation, McClane exacerbates the situation because he is too stubborn to admit he was wrong.

But the very same bold headedness that facilitated pushing his marriage into disarray might be the exact thing needed for McClane to save the day when a heavily armed team of tactical bad guys led by German radical Hans Gruber seize the tower and take everyone—except McClane—hostage.

And thus begins the premise of a ground-breaking movie that not only resulted in a film that the *New York Times* hailed as "the perfect movie for our time" but it revolutionized the cinematic landscape, creating a new sub-genre of action films, and resulted in breakthrough cinematic roles for actors Bruce Willis, Alan Rickman, and Reginald VelJohnson.

Die Hard premiered at the Avco Theatre in Los Angeles, California on July 12, 1988, followed by a slightly broader release on July 15th to twenty-one theatres in thirteen cities. A full release took place the following week on July 20, 1988, to 1,276 theaters.

The film earned $7.1 million, finishing in the number three spot for that weekend, behind *Who Framed Roger Rabbit* (The number one spot at $8.9 million) and *Coming to America* (in the number two spot at $8.8 million).

Though *Die Hard* never claimed the number one spot it spent ten straight weeks among the top five highest grossing movies. It ended the year earning a gross box office of somewhere between $81.3 and $83 million as the seventh highest grossing film of 1988.

The movie, directed by John McTiernan, and with a screenplay by Jeb Stuart and Steven E. de Souza, was adapted from

Roderick Thorp's 1979 action thriller *Nothing Lasts Forever*. It was a sequel to his 1966 novel *The Detective*.

Thorp's 1966 thriller/detective novel had been adapted into a 1968 movie of the same name staring Frank Sinatra in the lead role of private detective Joe Leland. The film was ranked as one of the highest grossing movies of 1968 and was also one of the biggest hits of Sinatra's career as an actor.

20th Century Fox purchased the sequel rights long before *Nothing Lasts Forever* had even been written. As such, there was a contractual right for the studio to offer the lead role in the film to Frank Sinatra. In his seventies at that time, Sinatra declined the role, which led to a series of other actors who were considered.

Even Bruce Willis, who was eventually offered the role had to initially decline due to contractual obligations to the television show he'd been staring in. It was only because of the pregnancy of his *Moonlighting* co-star Cybill Shepherd that they shut down the show for 11 weeks— enough time for Willis to parlay into being able to play the role of John McClane on the set of *Die Hard*.

Initial critical reviews of the movie were mixed—Roger Ebert dismissed the movie as "a mess" that "shoots itself in the foot"—but audiences were enthralled by the movie, with an average rating of "A+" in market research conducted by CinemaScore.

John McTiernan's work as a director was mostly praised. In a July 1988 review in the *Los Angeles Times*, Kevin Thomas described the commandeering of the skyscraper as a "textbook study of the process, as terrifyingly persuasive as it is swift." He went on to write that the movie is "a formidable introduction to the visual virtuosity of director John McTiernan and cinematographer Jan De Bont, who are backed spectacularly well by ingenious production designer Jackson DeGovia and a raft of special effects magicians."

There were also mixed reviews of lead actor Bruce Willis, including being described as "a bit pale and TV-tentative" (Dave Kehr, *Chicago Tribune*), but several reviewers praised his comedic range, and leading-man status. His casting was said to have brought a necessary vulnerability to a contemporary hero, one who is able to display fear, remorse, and indecision without being overly macho nor comedic.

Kevin Thomas of *Los Angeles Times* said that Willis's "terrific sense of humor makes him a star as much as his broad shoulders do." And in *The Washington Post* Hal Hinson raved about the "grace and physical bravado" that allows Willis to stand alongside the likes of contemporary action hero stars Sylvester Stallone and Arnold Schwarzeneggar.

Alan Rickman, who was already in his early 40's when he made his big screen debut with this film, was consistently praised. He was described as portraying "the perfect snake" by reviewer Caryn James, and his role as Hans Gruber was compared to Laurence Olivier's performance in the 1955 *Richard III*. Even Roger Eber, who mostly panned the film singled out Rickman's performance as the only credible one in the film.

The film was nominated for four different Academy Awards in 1989. Best Film

Editing (Frank J. Urioste and John F. Link); Best Visual Effects (Richard Edlund, Al DiSarro, Brent Boates, and Thaine Morris); Best Sound (Don J. Bassman, Kevin F. Cleary, Richard Overton, and Al Overton Jr.); and Best Sound Effects Editing (Stephen Hunter Flick and Richard Shorr). Michael Kamen won a BMI TV/Film Award for his work on the film's score.

Like a fine wine or barrel-aged whisky, the taste for this 1988 blockbuster summer film has improved with the passing of time. Over the years numerous publications, including *Entertainment Weekly*, *IGN*, and *Empire* have listed *Die Hard* as the greatest action film of all time. In 2017 the film was selected by the United States Library of Congress to be preserved in the National Film Registry for being "culturally, historically, or aesthetically significant."

While history has seemed to have settled the debate over the merits of the film, one debate that lives on is whether *Die Hard* is a Christmas movie.

But that's not the only thing that lives on in the hearts and minds of movie patrons.

Die Hard also kicked off a franchise of four movie sequels and spin-off products in other entertainment media that spanned more than 30 years and five decades.

A sixth entry into the series, under the various potential and speculated names of *Die Hardest*, *Die Hard, Year One*, *Old Habits Die Hard* and *McClane* did not come to pass due to a combination of factors. Despite Bruce Willis indicating his interest in reprising his role for the sixth and final entry in the franchise, in 2017 Disney acquired 21st Century Fox, and in 2022, Willis, who had been diagnosed with aphasia (an inability to communicate because of damage to specific brain regions) officially retired from acting.

Perhaps the way the building where *Die Hard* was set still stands out high in the sky like a beacon where Olympic Boulevard and Avenue of the Stars cross, a constant reminder of a movie that changed the face of action films, *Die Hard* itself towers in its way in the overall landscape of Hollywood.

The movie not only launched careers, and countless copycat and inspired pastiches, but it fueled endless other writers, directors, producers, and creators, reminding them there was constantly new ground to break in creative storytelling.

Regardless of all the spin-offs media tie-ins, and memes related to the movie, there's one thing that seems constant: the overall love that people have for the original *Die Hard* film.

Perhaps this is because, as Kim Taylor-Foster writes in her 2022 book *Why We Love Die Hard* that it isn't a typical action film, but instead, "a family drama, a Christmas movie, a satirical buddy cop comedy, and an action thriller all in one."

Die Hard is, at once, all these things, and more, holding a legacy that has proven itself to be, like its name implies, something that will continue to be around for a long time.

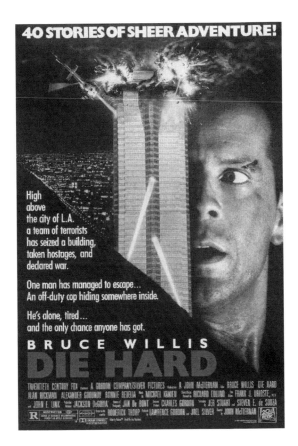

Bruce Willis, Die Hard (20th Century Fox, 1988). Poster
File Reference # 33595_863THA

BOOK 'EM

Nothing Lasts Forever, the Roderick
Thorp novel that inspired *Die Hard*

Die Hard was adapted from Roderick Thorp's *Nothing Lasts Forever*, an action-adventure thriller novel first published in 1979.

The novel was a sequel to Thorp's 1966 *The Detective* featuring retired NYPD Joe Leland who works as a private detective. That book was adapted into a 1968 neo-noir crime film of the same name starring Frank Sinatra. It was billed as "an adult look at a police detective" and addressed topics such as infidelity and homosexuality that had, at the time, been considered taboo for mainstream cinema.

Thorp wrote *Nothing Lasts Forever* based on a vivid dream he had on the night he had seen the 1974 movie *The Towering Inferno*. His dream was about a man being chased around a high-rise building by a group of gun-toting assailants.

In the novel, Joe Leland is in his sixties and retired from the NYPD and from his stint as a private detective. At Christmas, Leland flies to Los Angeles to visit his daughter, Stephanie Gennaro who works as an executive at the LA headquarters of the foreign owned company Klaxon-Oil.

Leland isn't at the Christmas party long before he starts to pick up on the fact that his daughter has been involved in some of the company's shadier business dealings. Weary, Leland excuses himself to visit the restroom, and following advice from a stranger on how to deal with jet lag, he removes his shoes, washes his feet, and walks around barefoot.

That's when the terrorist group breaks in and—from his hiding spot—Leland recognizes leader Anton Gruber, aka *Antonio Rojas* (Little Tony the Red). He also witnesses Gruber murder Klaxon's CEO, Mr. Rivers.

Armed with just his pistol, and barefoot, Leland hides, runs, climbs, crawls, and jumps about the office tower, exhausted and alone. He slowly picks off the terrorists one-by-one and sustains numerous injuries. Throughout the long night, he also passes the time by sleeping and reflecting on things such as his unfaithful wife and a cute flight attendant he had brief chemistry with on his way in from New York.

Getting his hands on a radio, Leland communicates with a young cop, Al Powell, and a CB radio enthusiast.

In his near-climactic confrontation with Gruber, Leland is unable to save his daughter Stephanie as she and the head terrorist dangle out the window, with Anton holding on to her wristwatch. The two both fall to their death.

Shortly after, one of the surviving terrorists, Karl, bursts through a staircase door in an attempt to kill Leland. While police captain Dwayne Robinson is shot dead in the encounter, Leland's confidante, Al Powell kills Karl with a single shot.

As you can see, there were numerous elements of the story that were revised for the film. It's important to note how the novel's concept, the action taking place over a single day, the noir elements, and even Thorp's depiction of a cynical hero who speaks in punchy, sharp, hard-boiled lines had an effect on parallel elements in the blockbuster film.

Jeb Stuart was approached by producer Lawrence Gordon and Lloyd Levin to adapt Thorp's novel into a screenplay. And, though he needed the work, and was eager to get this screenplay done, he struggled with the grim and cynical tone of the novel, the sad ending, and the fact the action hero was in his sixties.

It wasn't until he got into a huge fight with his wife before storming out the door to drive back to his office that things fell into place for Stuart.

As he explains in the season 1, episode 4 of *The Movies That Made Us*, he was speeding on his way to the office, and distracted with how he was going to apologize to his wife because he knew that she was right, when he was caught off guard by a huge refrigerator box that had fallen from a truck onto the lane in front of him. Unable to avoid it, he drove right through it at sixty-five miles an hour, thinking that this was the end for him.

Relieved, and with his heart pounding he suddenly *knew* what the story was. "It's not about a sixty-year-old man who drops his daughter off a building, it's about a thirty-year-old who should have said he's sorry to his wife and something really bad happens."

Freshly inspired, Stuart wrote thirty-five pages of the script that night. And though he'd never written an action script before, he was familiar with thrillers. So he used that. He also adapted experience from friends who had been going through separation and divorce to come up with the element of Holly reverting to her maiden name, further setting off John's stubborn anger.

Stuart also made notable changes to the supporting cast of characters, making their roles far more important, and allowing McClane to interact with them to draw out his humanity, his flaws, and his anger. He gave the limousine driver a name and had his role continue throughout the film. Also, Al Powell became a husband and father, so that the bond between McClane and Powell could be tighter.

The screenwriter also incorporated elements of a Western theme throughout the story, in a suggestion that John McClane was a modern-day cowboy.

Several other influences ended up readapting the script. Joel Silver insisted that the top of the building had to blow up, and director John McTiernan refused to direct a movie that was about terrorists. He insisted that terrorism was not entertaining, but that everybody loves a good caper.

And, late in the process, just as filming was going to begin, producer Joel Silver brought Steven E. de Souza on board to make further revisions to the script. As John McTiernan explains, the humor Bruce Willis displayed in the television show *Moonlighting* worked well; but on the big screen that smart-ass stuff they'd been doing didn't work.

Among those revisions were the addition of more quips from McClane's character. This came from a meeting that de Souza had with Willis on the set, with both agreeing it would work better to integrate more humor.

The other thing the two discussed during that meeting was their mutual love, as children, of *The Roy Rogers Show*. That's where the line that transcends the film (and was used for the title of this book) came from.

In 1988 *Nothing Lasts Forever* was released under the title *DIE HARD*TM complete with the font used in the movie title and the little "TM" (Trademark) designating it was a Trademark of Twentieth Century Fox Film Corp. and the disclaimer reading: 'Formerly titled: Nothing Lasts Forever.'

In 2012, *Nothing Lasts Forever* was brought back into print. It was simultaneously released as an eBook for the 24th anniversary of the movie.

THE COPY

Here is the back cover copy that appears on the 1979 first edition of *Nothing Lasts Forever*.

Rave reviews for
The Detective
By Roderick Thorp

"What John Le Carré did for the dirty business of spying, Thorp has done for the dreary business of private-eying."

—Chicago Tribune

"An absorbing story laced with suspense and surprise. . . . Thorp has grasped what so many novelists have long neglected, namely, the undeveloped potential of the novel of detection."

—John Barkham

"This book is an original. It is daring. . . . Our fictional private eyes usually come with skins like crocodiles. Detective Joe Leland is something else: a scarred, vibrating received of psychic hurts, remorseless in his pursuit of hidden meanings."

—San Francisco Examiner

"An astounding climax. . . . The author has a vast knowledge of the intricacies of the human mind, its frailties and its strength."

— Boston Herald

"A big, sprawling book, expansive in invention, opulent in detail . . . a surprising and explosive ending."

— *New York Times*

And here is the copy that appears on the inner leaf jacket of that same edition.

Nothing Lasts Forever
Roderick Thorp

Here is Roderick Thorp's breathtakingly fast-paced sequel to his electrifying bestseller *The Detective*

The setting: Los Angeles; the time: those precious twenty-four hours that span Christmas Eve and Christmas morning.

Joe Leland, veteran cop, former war hero, expert on the evils and violence of the world, steps into the most terrifying situation any policeman ever has to face—a crime in progress. Cut off, high in an office building under the sallow southern California sky, Leland finds himself in a fight to the death with a dozen foreign terrorists while the lives of seventy-five hostages, including his own daughter and grandchildren, hang in the balance.

Flying in to visit his family for the holidays, Leland is whisked by limousine from LAX to the building of Klaxon Oil, where his daughter is a high-powered executive. It is an oil company, true, but to Leland's practiced eye obviously something more, and within minutes after his arrival the Klaxon building is invaded by a force even more sinister and violent—a dozen young Germans armed with machine guns and high explosives, bent on destruction and death.

Because he is a police expert, an advisor and consultant to governments and corporations around the world, Leland knows the terrorists and what they're capable of—but he knows, too, the destruction of potential of the antiterrorist contingency plans of the Los Angeles Police Department.

Alone, caught between forces and people he despises equally, Leland soon realizes that if he is to live, others must die. Before dawn of Christmas day, all Los Angeles knows that a small, inaccessible war is being fought at the top of the Klaxon building. By daylight, via television, the whole world is watching.

The Detective was recognized as "bold, daring an inventive, the first claim for the detective story as literature since Raymond Chandler." This novel makes the same claim for the contemporary thriller.

[Author Photo of Roderick Thorp]

Born and raised in New York City, Roderick Thorp now lives in Los Angeles, where he writes not only novels—this is his seventh—but also non-fiction books and articles. He is best known for *The Detective*, an international best seller and motion picture, and a forerun of *Nothing Lasts Forever*.

ABOUT RODERICK THORP

Roderick Mayne Thorp Jr. (Sept 1, 1936 – April 28, 1999) was an American novelist who specialized mainly in novels that involved police procedure, crime, and thrillers.

Thorp was born in the Bronx. He went to City College of New York—where he won several prizes for his short story writing—and graduated in 1957. Shortly after graduating from college, he worked at a detective agency owned by his father. When his father retired, Thorp took over the operation for a couple of years, continuing to learn about investigative techniques and police procedures.

Thorp's first novel, *Into the Forest*, which was released in 1961, did not sell very well. But his second novel, *The Detective*, was a bestseller, selling millions of copies worldwide and generating a windfall of royalties. Further royalties would come in after the adaption of *The Detective* and *Nothing Lasts Forever* into blockbuster films and his novels *Rainbow Drive* and *Devlin* were adapted into TV movies.

Thorp described himself as a "seat of the pants" writer to the *Los Angeles Times*, and his son Roddy Thorp told *The Times* in a May 1999 article that up until he started to suffer from arthritis, his father would write the first drafts of his novel longhand with a No. 2 pencil and loose-leaf paper.

In addition to his detective agency work and writing, Thorp taught literature and lectured on creative writing at various schools and even, later in life, online where he mentored fledging writers. He taught at Ramapo College in New Jersey, and in 1976 moved to Los Angeles where he also did newspaper work, including a 21-part series for the Los Angeles Herald Examiner called "On the Cocaine Trail."

Despite the success from his books and the adaptions they inspired, Thorp remained an unassuming man. He was quoted in a May 1999 *Los Angeles Times* article as saying: "The quality of my life isn't in shopping for gold-plated cars. I value friendship, loyalty, truthfulness, honor—you know, the intrinsics that seem to have gone by the board. . . . I don't care whether the neighbors know I've made it or not."

Thorp died of a heart attack at the age of 62 in Oxnard, California in 1999 and was survived by his wife Claudia, his sons Roddy and Stephen, and his grandchildren Stacey, Valerie, and Carolyn.

BIBLIOGRAPHY:

- Into the Forest (1961)
- The Detective (1966)
- Dionysus (1969)
- The Music of Their Laughter: An American Album (1970)
- Wives: An Investigation (1971)
- Slaves (1973)
- The Circle of Love (1974)
- Westfield (1977)
- Nothing Lasts Forever (1979) (reissued as Die Hard)
- Jenny and Barnum: A Novel of Love (1981)
- Rainbow Drive (1986)
- Devlin (1988)
- River: A Novel of the Green River Killings (1995)

SAY IT AIN'T JOE

When working on the screenplay, writers Jeb Stuart and Steven E. de Souza had to make several important adaptations and adjustments, either of their own volition, or in collaboration with producer Joel Silver and director John McTiernan.

Here's a summary of some of the changes made between the book and the movie.

Novel	Movie
Nothing Lasts Forever	Die Hard
Joe Leland	John McClane
Protagonist's age: 60s	Protagonist's age: 30s
Joe's daughter Stephanie Gennaro	John's wife Holly Gennaro-McClane
Anton Gruber	Hans Gruber
Terrorists	Robbers masquerading as terrorists
Klaxon Oil	Nakatomi Corporation
Mr. Rivers (CEO)	Joseph Yoshinobu Takagi (head executive)
CB enthusiast Taco Bill	TV news reporter Richard Thornburg
Unnamed Chauffeur	Argyle
Note on bad guy Tony's sweater: NOW WE HAVE A MACHINE GUN	NOW I HAVE A MACHINE GUN HO-HO-HO
Joe's daughter dies when she falls off the building with Gruber	John manages to save his wife Holly
Deputy Chief of Police Dwayne Robinson is killed when shot by Karl	Dwayne Robinson does not get shot and survives

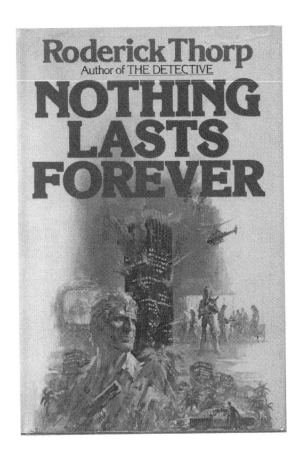

The front cover of the original hardcover edition of
Roderick Thorp's *Nothing Lasts Forever* from the author's
personal collection.

RODERICK THORP

Author of RAINBOW DRIVE

Twelve terrorists. One cop.
The odds are against him...
That's just the way he likes it.

DIE HARD™

Now a major motion picture from Twentieth Century Fox Film Corp.

Formerly titled: NOTHING LASTS FOREVER

0229-5 (Canada \$6.95) U.S. \$4.95

Front cover of the August 1988 mass market re-released paperback edition (also known as the "movie tie-in edition") of the Ivy Books / Ballantine Books *Die Hard* (Formerly titled: *Nothing Lasts Forever*) from the author's personal collection.

NEW YORK TIMES BESTSELLING AUTHOR

RODERICK THORP

BASIS FOR THE FILM
DIE HARD
25th ANNIVERSARY

NOTHING LASTS FOREVER

Front cover of the Graymalkin Media edition of the book, published in 2013 for the 25th Anniversary of the release of *Die Hard*. Book cover design by Ervin Serrano and David Zendel. From the author's personal collection.

FURTHER ADAPTATIONS

Sources for the other movies in the *Die Hard* franchise

*N*othing Lasts Forever wasn't the only text that had been reconceived and adapted into a script for the *Die Hard* franchise. There was at least one other book and an article in *Wired* magazine that acted as inspirational sources for the next two films.

DIE HARDER: DIE HARD 2

58 Minutes by Walter Wager became the basis for *Die Harder: Die Hard 2*. Screenwriter Doug Richardson had started working on it within the first few weeks of the release of *Die Hard* under the direction of producer Lawrence Gordon.

In *58 Minutes* NYPD officer Frank Malone waits at JFK airport in New York for his daughter who is flying in to visit him for Christmas. A blizzard moves in just as terrorists take over air traffic control. Malone has less than an hour to figure out a way to save everyone, including his daughter.

In the early phases of Doug Richardson's adaptation, he changed the name of the book's hero from Frank Malone to Frank Zelinski. He was under directions from Larry Gordon who was planning on producing this sequel film with his brother Charles rather than with Joel Silver.

The movie did end up being produced by Charles Gordon, Lawrence Gordon and Joel Silver, and, as the Gordon's knew would happen, Silver brought in script writer Steven de Souza to draft further rewrites of the screenplay.

Not only did de Souza re-adapt Wager's main character into John McClane, but he changed the daughter into McClane's wife Holly Gennaro. He also re-worked the main antagonist, Willi Staub, into Colonel William Stuart, an ex-US Special Forces commander turned mercenary who was hired to free General Ramon Esperanza. JFK airport was changed to Dulles Inter-

national Airport in Washington, DC, and
Carmine Lorenzo (Dennis Franz), head of
airport security, became this film's version
of Deputy Chief Dwayne Robinson—an
uncooperative local law enforcement figure.

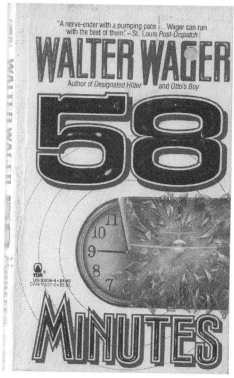

Front cover of *58 Minutes* by Walter Wager, 1989,
Tor Books. From the author's personal collection.

Silver also insisted that they find a way to fit Al Powell into the script. Actor Reginald VelJohnson was already in the process of shooting the first season of the television program *Family Matters*, but the executives were flexible enough to allow him the leeway to shoot two small scenes for *Die Hard 2*.

William Atherton, who played television reporter Richard Thornburg, was brought on, which created a fascinating parallel storyline as he and Holly Gennaro were trapped on the same airplane, with some very memorable conflict between the two.

A major change Steven de Souza introduced was the sequence where McClane is unable to stop the terrorists from deliberately crashing an airplane on the runway. But apart from the ploy to "totally-mind-fuck the audience" as de Souza put it, it served an important storytelling purpose. It demonstrated that McClane could make mistakes and fail; and it left him vulnerable and wounded.

Renny Harlin was brought on as director immediately after finishing work in

August 1989 of the movie *Ford Fairlane*. One of the many important actions Harlin took was convincing actor Bruce Willis, who wanted the humor removed from his character, that it would be a huge mistake. Harlin explained that the reason the audience loved *Die Hard* is because it was a blue-collar guy with marital problems who has a wry and witty sense of humor.

DIE HARD WITH A VENGEANCE

At one point, a script entitled *Troubleshooter* with McClane fighting terrorists on a Caribbean Cruise, had been considered for the third film in the franchise. Producer Gordon had also commissioned another adaptation from a different Walter Wager book—Wager's *58 Minutes* had been adapted into *Die Hard 2*—that was set on a British ocean liner. This story saw John and Holly on a vacation bound for Italy to rekindle their romance when terrorists smuggle atomic weapon detonators aboard.

Both scripts were rejected for being too similar to the 1992 Steven Seagal film *Un-*

der Siege. The script that had been called *Troubleshooter* was later adapted into what became *Speed 2: Cruise Control*.

The third *Die Hard* movie was eventually based on a spec script Hensleigh had originally conceived as a Brandon Lee action film before the actor's death, with the working title *Simon Says*. The script was considered for the fourth installment of the Lethal Weapon series before being picked up for the *Die Hard* franchise.

Simon Says centered on a NYPD police officer forced into a partnership with a reluctant shopkeeper to take on a villain who is terrorizing the city with a series of devastating bombs.

LIVE FREE OR DIE HARD

The script entitled *Tears of the Sun*—*Die Hard* in the jungle—was initially considered for the fourth installment of the movie franchise. This script was rejected, but Willis later stared in a 2003 movie of the same name as a non-McClane character.

Writer David Marconi crafted a script entitled *WW3* that was based on a May 1,

1997, *Wired* magazine article written by John Carlin about the possibility of a major cyber attack on US soil. You can read the article in its entirety on the *Wired* website at this link:

https://www.wired.com/1997/05/netizen-2/

A GOOD DAY TO DIE HARD

Unlike the previous films, the script for the fifth movie in the franchise wasn't adapted from an existing book, article, or screenplay script. Skip Woods, who worked with Bruce Willis on his dialogue in *Live Free or Die Hard* was hired to write the script.

Like in all the previous films, additional tweaking of the script continued during production. Director John Moore was finessing elements of the screenplay as filming approached, and Jason Keller was brought in to do an uncredited rewrite of the script. Keller was given an executive producer credit for that work.

BEYOND THE BIG SCREEN

Die Hard's reach into other formats,
other media, and pop culture

*D*ie Hard was initially spun off of a single novel and into a franchise that has spanned over five decades, but it is also responsible for a significant number of its own spin-offs.

Apart from the re-release, and even reprinting of a couple of the novels that inspired two of the movies in the franchise in what the book industry often refers to as "movie-tie-in" editions, the world of *Die Hard* has also extended into other books, comics, board games, video games, toys and action figures, music, and theatrical performances.

Within months of the release of *Die Hard* in 1988, the video game company Mediagenic licensed the first *Die Hard* game. It was released in 1990 and offered a few firsts of its kind in the video game realm. Instead of forcing the player into fixed tasks, it was more of what's known in the industry as a "sandbox" game. Players could move freely around the environment, either engaging with or avoiding enemies of their own volition.

There was also limited ammunition without an on-screen ammo counter. In addition, unlike most other games of the time, the player would only get a single life. Die once and the game was over. These elements added to the tension in the game play.

Fox Interactive released *Die Hard Trilogy* in 1996, a game developed by Probe Entertainment, a UK-based game company. This game allowed players into the "plots" of the first three films in the franchise. The first was a third-person shooter set in Nakatomi Plaza. The second, set in Dules Airport, was a first-person shooter. And the third featured driving action as the player raced around New York City in an attempt to diffuse bombs. This game was banned in Germany for violence because of the fact players could drive their vehicle into and kill innocent pedestrians.

In 2000, the same company released a far-less successful sequel to the game entitled *Die Hard Trilogy 2: Viva Las Vegas*. This game, developed by American video game company n-Space, featured the three similar scenarios of third-person shooter, first-person shooter, and action driving.

In 2002 Fox Interactive released *Die Hard: Vendetta*, which was developed by Bits Studios. Set five years after the events of *Die Hard with a Vengeance*, this first-person shooter game features the voice of Reginald VelJohnson in the role of Al Powell, and McClane's daughter Lucy as a member of the Los Angeles Police Department.

A few unique elements of this game include puzzle-like elements that the player, as McClane, has to solve, the fact McClane can take his own hostages, communication with other Non-Player Characters, a "bullet-time" effect (made popular in the *Max Payne* videogames), and a game feature called "Hero Time." Players have to earn this ability by performing heroic actions. When in Hero Time mode—which allows the action to slow down so the player can better manipulate difficult stunts, such as saving hostages— Beethoven's "Ode to Joy" plays.

Sega's 1996 *Die Hard Arcade* was published in cooperation with Fox Interactive. But because Sega did not have Japanese rights to the franchise, in Japan it was released as *Dynamite Deka* (Dynamite Detective).

Other video games created over the years include *Die Hard: Nakatomi Plaza* (2002) as well as a series of games created specifically for use on mobile phones, including the 2013 *Die Hard* where players take the role of Jack McClane—John's son from *A Good Day to Die Hard*.

In 2005 Palisades created a series of fourteen cute articulated plastic figures in their Die Hard PALz series. The fourteen figures include (in alphabetical order): Agent Johnson, Argyle, Ellis, Hans Gruber, Hans Gruber (Showdown), Holly Gennero, John McClane, John McClane (Showdown), John McClane (Yippie-Kay-Yay), Karl, Sgt Al Powell, Special Agent Johnson, Tony, and Tony (Ho-Ho-Ho). Of note, Argyle comes with a teddy bear, Al Powell comes with a Twinkie, and one version of Tony includes him in a chair with the Christmas greeting written on his sweater. At the time of this writing, I found listings for these characters priced anywhere from $20 for a single character through to $1000 USD for a full set, with several listings around $200 to $400.

In 2006, the National Entertainment Collectibles Association released as part of their Cult Classics series, a seven-inch-tall bare foot John McClane action figure complete with his white blood-stained t-shirt, an MP5 submachine gun, and a rooftop base stand.

In 2013 at their eleventh 'Mystery Movie' event in Los Angeles, Mondo released a special poster created by Laurent Durieux that depicts Nakatomi Plaza inside a broken snow globe. It was given away to one lucky participant at the event which featured a 35 MM screening of *Die Hard*, prop detonators located throughout the location, fake broken glass strewn about the theatre floor, and was attended by actor Reginald VelJohnson, who played Al Powell.

Yippee Ki-Yay Merry Christmas: A Die Hard Musical Parody debuted November 29, 2014 at MCL Chicago. MCL Chicago is a storefront theatre that was founded in July of that same year by Stephanie McCullough, Michael Shepherd Jordan, and Alex Garday to celebrate the art of music comedy, improv, musical improv, and musical theater. In late September, only having been open three months, the founders realized they needed a show for the Fall/Winter season. Acting volunteer secretary at the time, Alex Richmond, mentioned that her family watched *Die Hard* every holiday season and as mentioned on their website "the C4 was set, so to speak." The founders quickly went to work parodying the beloved 80s action movie, turning it into a hilarious musical still loved by people to this day.

This unauthorized musical parody of the 1988 film classic is in no way affiliated with 20th Century Fox or any associated entities involved in the film. But the creators knew they had a hit and continued to edit, develop, and update the show each year. Core cast members returned, and more importantly, audiences returned. The show has developed some die hard "Yippee Ki-Yay Merry Christmas" fans, and every year audience members come back to discover what fun new jokes, songs, or bits the creative team has in store. In fact, some audience members have seen the show every year— sometimes multiple times per year— bringing friends and family members to experience the holiday tradition.

Yippee has run every holiday season since 2014 and expanded each year until the global pandemic of 2020. It is also available for theatre companies to license.

A performance from the 2018-2019 season was recorded in front of a live sold-out audience by Sam Bowers at The Den Theatre in Chicago and is available to view for free online in a YouTube video that premiered December 17, 2020. You can find the video here:

https://www.youtube.com/@YippeeTheMusical

In 2022 *Yippee Ki Yay*, a one-man poetry action stage show parody re-telling of the classic tale written and performed by Richard Marsh premiered at Edinburgh Fringe. Marsh, a Fringe First-winner, London poetry slam champion, and BBC Audio Drama Best Scripted Comedy Drama award-winner has received critical acclaim for this show. *The Guardian* says that "whether you're a *Die Hard* fan or not, it guarantees happy trails." And *The Times* called it "epically entertaining."

In a YouTube trailer for the Seabright Productions show, Marsh can be seen sharing a few key moments from the show, including a part where he says: "So this is the time and this is the place, for John to be hit very hard in the face."

But what about the world of books—you know, the place where the original source material for the script that became *Die Hard* originated?

For all fans, as I mentioned in my intro-duction, I highly recommend two specific books.

The first, *Die Hard: The Ultimate Visual History* written by James Mottram and

David S. Cohen, released by Insight Editions in 2018, is a gorgeous coffee-table sized hardcover that celebrates the entire franchise, including in depth details about the making of each film, and a wealth of rare and unseen imagery, set photography, and concept art.

The second is Running Press's 2022 book *Why We Love Die Hard* by Kim Taylor-Foster. This book, dramatically illustrated by Ink Bad Company, explores why this classic movie continues to hold up and how it became a pop culture touchstone.

Doogie Horner, a huge *Die Hard* fan has released a number of books related to his admiration for the movie.

In 2016 Horner released a coloring book authorized by 20th Century Fox called *Die Hard: The Authorized Color and Activity Book*. Some of the movie's best moments are captured in a way that fans can savor their favorite scenes and quotes in a fresh and creative way.

Because Horner is in the camp of people who believe that *Die Hard* is a Christmas movie, he rewrote it into a children's picture book illustrated by JJ Harrison in 2017. For *A Die Hard Christmas*, Horner merged the action of this holiday classic with the holiday poem *A Visit From St. Nicholas* (commonly knowns as *'Twas The Night Before Christmas*).

Response to Horner's book was huge, and it continues to be re-shared every Christmas season on social media. Screenwriter Steven de Souza said, on Twitter that the book settled, for once and for all, the argument about *Die Hard* being a Christmas movie. As of the writing of this book, it has more than 3,200 reviews on Amazon with a 4.9 out of 5 rating. And on Goodreads, is has more than 1,200 ratings with a 4.6 average.

In my household, reading and displaying that book for guests to marvel over is an annual tradition, along with watching *Die Hard*, *Die Hard 2*, *Elf*, and *National Lampoon's Christmas Vacation*.

As a special present for his friends and family, Horner combined what he says are the two best Christmas films into a novella called *Home Alone Hard*.

Here is the premise for the book:

John McClane is one of Chicago's finest cops, but he's a lousy husband. On the morning of his family's big vacation to the West Coast, he oversleeps, and his frustrated wife, Holly, leaves without him.

When John wakes up in an empty house, a series of unfortunate events leads him to believe that he made his family disappear.

Overcome with grief and regret, John doesn't call the cops when a pair of German burglars start casing his home; a good fight is just what he's looking for. Welcome to the party, pal.

You can listen to the entire nearly 2-hour reading of the book on Horner's YouTube channel. You can also download the eBook or the audiobook for free on Horner's website.

https://www.doogiehorner.com/homealonehard/

In addition, on Horner's website he says that the main character in his young adult novel *This Might Hurt a Bit* features a main character that has an unhealthy obsession with the film. The moment I found this out, I immediately bought myself a copy of the book.

In my own novel *Fear and Longing in Los Angeles* my main character, Michael Andrews, a fan of Spider-Man is also a fan of the *Die Hard* franchise. While at Newark International Airport, Michael is enjoying breakfast at a crowded bar seat beside a beautiful young woman. Their conversation about classic films leads to a discussion about *Die Hard*, which they both adore, and Michael begins to riff on trivia related to the film. When she comes on to him, Michael, still entangled in a complicated relationship, adapts a line from *Die Hard 2* and says "Just the flapjacks, ma'am." Later in that same novel, Andrews is also delighted that the young limo driver sent to pick him up from the airport looks a little like the actor De'voreaux White and goes by the nickname Argyle.

But John McClane has also appeared in comic book formats. Published between September 2009 and April 2010, BOOM! Studios released a series entitled *Die Hard: Year One*. This eight-issue series written by Howard Chaykin was released in two volumes.

Volume One is set in 1976 and follows John McClane's adventures as a rookie cop in New York City. Volume Two takes place in 1977 during the famous city-wide black-out.

In 2018, in time for the thirtieth anniversary of the start of the franchise, Insight Comics published *A Million Ways to Die Hard* written by Frank Tieri and illustrated by Mark Texeira.

Set thirty years after the events of Christmas Eve at Nakatomi Plaza, it features an older McClane forced to return to the original setting to face down a movie-fanatic terrorist who has kidnapped his ex-wife Holly and other hostages. The book includes McClane meeting Cam Powell, Al Powell's son, Hideki Tagaki, son of Joseph Takagi, Elsa Gruber, sister of Hans Gruber.

It's a safe bet, of course, that there will continue to be further *Die Hard* inspired properties that go well beyond what we've already seen in the past thirty-five years.

ANOTHER ORPHAN OF A BANKRUPT CULTURE

Why do we love John McClane?

The character of John McClane that we know and love to this day—and who is virtually synonymous with actor Bruce Willis—certainly didn't start off that way.

For one, the character name was made up for the script that became *Die Hard*. McClane was based on Joe Leland, from the source material novel *Nothing Lasts Forever* by Roderick Thorp.

In that novel, Leland was a sixty-year-old retired NYPD detective. He is depicted as emotionally shattered from his experiences as a fighter pilot in WWII, his failed marriage, and the death of his ex-wife.

Leland appeared in Thorp's 1966 novel *The Detective* which was adapted into a film of the same name in 1968 starring Frank Sinatra as Leland.

As scriptwriter Jeb Stuart was adapting the film, he needed to make the character younger, and changed the Gennaro character to the protagonist's wife rather than his daughter.

He also renamed the character, as part of ensuring this adaptation was a standalone and not seen as a sequel to the 1969 film.

One of the initial names he came up with was John Ford, partly as a nod to the legendary film director. But the powers that be felt the name was too important in the history of cinema to be used in an action movie.

That's when Stuart drew upon his own Celtic roots and went with the surname McClane.

Because of a contract clause Sinatra had the right of first refusal of the lead role in any film adaptation of *Nothing Lasts Forever*. Sinatra turned it down, allegedly stating that he was too old and too rich to play the role.

The role was then offered to a number of actors that included Clint Eastwood, Arnold Schwarzeneggar, Mel Gibson, Sylvester Stallone, James Caan, and Richard Gere.

When it was eventually offered to Bruce Willis, he had to initially turn it down due to his obligations on the television series *Moonlighting*. The pregnancy of his co-star Cybil Shepherd allowed him the opportunity to finally accept. But Willis's requirement to juggle responsibilities for the TV show and the action film meant that the script needed to be modified and leverage more use of several of the supporting characters. This led to enhancing the roles of Holly Gennaro, Al Powell, Argyle, Richard Thornberg, and Hans Gruber.

McClane becomes a much more realized and realistic character because of his relationship with these and other characters in the film. But what is it about him that makes him stand out?

First, he is vulnerable. We can see that from the very first shot of McClane in the film—his white-knuckled grip on the armrest as his flight lands in LA.

Shortly after, he admits to Argyle that he's hoping to make amends with the wife he is separated from. And, after getting into an argument with Holly, he derides himself for the immature way he handled the conversation.

Still later, as he is talking to Al on the radio, not sure if he's going to make it, he breaks down, his voice cracking, as he asks his partner to relay a message of apology to his wife. He wants her to know he recognizes where and how he screwed up and is sorry.

Second, McClane is a blue-collar, average guy who doesn't put on airs. This is seen in the way he dresses, in how he reacts to a fancy drink when he first arrives at the Christmas party, and the fact he rides in the front seat with his limo driver.

Third is his disdain for authority, pretension, and bullshit. But he doesn't rally against the rules for the sake of stirring the plot. It becomes clear that his rebellion is against those who flaunt or have a thirst for power.

McClane aligns himself with working-class folks like Al Powell and Argyle, while sneering at characters like Ellis, Dept Chief Dwayne Robinson, and the teenage boy style dick-swinging FBI Agents.

His relationship with Hans Gruber is a little more complicated. While he does have contempt for his nemesis, McClane recognizes the nuances, multiple layers, and intelligence of the man. There is an element of respect underlying the verbal jabs and digs he makes to his foe.

And that's where the final element of McClane's sardonic and wry humor bring all of this together. He relays a verbal assault against Gruber and others in the film, leveraging it like a weapon that nobody can ever remove from him. In his unpretentious way, McClane tells it like it is. This same trait which can derail his relationship with his wife can also be leveraged to taunt and mock the bad guys throughout the film.

It is ultimately McClane's use of words and humor and "sleight-of-mouth" as Kim Taylor-Foster calls it in her book *Why We Love Die Hard* that allows him to get the upper hand in the final climactic scene in the film. As Taylor-Foster also puts it "the mouth is mightier than the gun."

Prior to John McClane, big budget action movie stars were always larger than life muscle-bound macho men. McClane changed the scrip, showing the merits of a hero who was fallible, emotional, and loyal, compensating for his shortcomings, vulnerability, and fears with humor. As a life-long fan of *Spider-Man* and Peter Parker—who wise-cracks while fighting bad guys—it's no surprise to me that I immediately took a shine to this action hero.

McClane was an underdog who didn't seek out any of what went down. He was in town to apologize to his wife, and heroically stepped up to the occasion when nasty shit started happening around him.

As he tells his pal Al on the radio, all things being equal, he'd rather be in Philadelphia.

But as fans, we appreciate the fact that we get to watch this everyman not only rise up against all odds to save the day, but that he gets to make nice with his estranged wife, and "drive off" into the proverbial sunset with her at the end.

AN EXCEPTIONAL THIEF

Why Gruber is Hans-down such a fantastic
and memorable villain

Hans Gruber was the perfect nemesis for John McClane. But he didn't always start off that way.

In the original version of the script, Gruber's character was depicted as more of a downscale villain.

But with McClane's character being modified from the originally written suave and sophisticated hero to a "working-class" everyman, director John McTiernan wanted to contrast that with an "upper-class" villain.

Gruber dresses, speaks, and behaves like a proper English gentleman throughout the movie, with an expensive taste in fashion and riffing on lines from the classics. The only time he breaks from this is in reaction to being taunted by John McClane.

Gruber is well educated, slick, and sophisticated, and he makes sure to con-

stantly remind people of this, never stray-
ing from boasting about his exceptionally
devious plan in orchestrating the heist.

And, while he does not hesitate to rack
up the body count on his way to fulfilling
the goal of the elaborate robbery scheme,
he conducts himself with poise, and even
shows respect for those he stands against.

Alan Rickman, who had never appeared
in a feature film before was initially hesi-
tant to play the bad guy in an action movie. But when he accepted, he approached
the role in a fresh way. The actor never
really saw Hans Gruber as the villain in
the film; but rather someone who had a
clear goal of what he wanted with a de-
tailed and carefully crafted plan to get it.

Though Gruber was elite, arrogant, and
sophisticated, Rickman recognized that
the key to the film was the mutual respect
Gruber and McClane have for one another, despite their differences. "I always
thought that was key," Rickman said. "I
think they're cut from the same cloth."

As a bit of an outsider himself, Gruber
also plays a role in standing outside
American society and making jagged
comments about it. He addresses the ills

of corporate greed (in a role that perhaps foreshadows the actor's own scene-stealing role as the Sheriff in 1991's *Robin Hood: Prince of Thieves*), shares his disdain for American culture which he describes as "bankrupt" and mocks the country's affection for "cowboy" action heroes.

In the same way Gruber respects the "fly in his ointment" he also shows a similar respect for Holly Gennaro. This is likely because she never backs down when confronting him.

There is a powerful moment between the two where, as Gruber is about to escort Mr. Takagi away, he makes eye contact with Gennaro, seemingly recognizing the inherent strength and power in her.

And later, when Gennaro, the calm-headed leader confronts him in the office to request a more comfortable accommodation for the pregnant woman and that the hostages need to use the restroom, the verbal sparring between the two begins.

When Gruber asks what idiot put her in charge she responds with: "You did. When you killed my boss."

Gruber, who was only partially attending to the interruption, immediately snaps his head up and looks at her, recognizing, again, something powerful in her that he respects.

Holly does not back down, even insults him without breaking eye contact, and after she makes her demands for the benefit of her colleagues, he responds with: "Yes, you're right. It will be done."

Near the end of the film, when she witnesses the real reason behind the invasion and occupation of Nakatomi Plaza, she calls him out.

"After all your posturing, all your little speeches," she says incredulously, "you're nothing but a common thief."

His response continues to display both his respect for her and his boastful nature. "I am an exceptional thief, Mrs. McClane," he says, getting right up in her face. "And since I'm moving up to kidnapping, you should be more polite."

Like in that first non-verbal glance between the two of them, Gennaro doesn't back down.

You can hear, a little later, as McClane is making his way to them, Holly yelling to him: "What are you going to do? Sit here while the building falls down around your ears?"

Gruber yells back at her in indecipherable German, but it's obvious that Gennaro, like McClane, has gotten to him with her own verbal sparring.

Hans Gruber repeatedly appears in various lists of the best movie villains of all time. He is listed, for example at #4 in *Empire Online's* October 23, 2022, article "The Best Movie Villains of All Time." He shares similarities to the eloquent, intelligent, and elitist characters of Hannibal Lecter and Darth Vader.

But if you consider movie villains from most other thrillers at the time, can you even name one other? For example, who were the bad guys in the *Lethal Weapon* movies of the 80s? Who did action heroes like Clint Eastwood, Sylvester Stallone, or Jean-Claude Van Damme face off against in *The Dead Pool, First Blood*, or *Bloodsport*?

Gruber was such an important nemesis for John McClane that he (or at least his memory and essence) was resurrected in the creation of the character of his brother Simon Gruber, as played by Jeremy Irons in the third film in the franchise.

SO WHAT DO I CALL YOU?

The origin of the phrase *Die Hard*

Apart from *Die Hard* being used for the popular John McClane related franchise and as a way to quickly describe other movies or storylines (The 1994 movie *Speed* is *Die Hard* on a bus), the term has been in use for a long time.

It was first coined in 1811 by British Army Officer William Inglis during the Battle of Albuera in the Peninsular War.

The Peninsular War was a military conflict fought in the Iberian Peninsula by Spain, Portugal, and the United Kingdom between 1807 and 1814. They were fighting the occupying and invading forces of the First French Empire during the Napoleonic Wars, which ran 1803 to 1815.

In May of 1811, during the Battle of Albuera, Lieutenant-Colonel William Inglis of the 57th (West Middlesex) Regiment of Foot was wounded by canister shot. Though injured, Inglis refused to give up. Instead of retiring from battle he remained with his regiment and in the midst of intense pressure from a French attack, encouraged his men with the words "Die hard 57th, die hard!"

The West Middlesex's regiment subsequently became known by the nickname the Die Hards.

The term was later used to describe senior officers of the Army who resisted military reform in the 1860s.

In British politics, the phrase *die-hard*, as an adjective, was used during the crisis caused by the Lords' rejection of David Lloyd George's "People's Budget" of 1909, to describe those who refused to accept the diminution of the House of Lords' powers by the Parliament Act 1911.

It was subsequently used to describe particular members of the Conservative Party in the 1930s and right-wing politics in general.

DieHard is, of course, a well-known US brand of automotive battery first produced in 1967. According to details on "The Diehard Legacy" section of the diehard.com website, it took nine years of intense research and more than one million dollars for Sears to develop "America's most innovative automotive battery —tested, proven and guaranteed to deliver across any circumstance."

Designed to produce 35% more useable starting power than other similar batteries, featuring a tough, thin-walled case of translucent polypropylene plastic, 50% percent thinner than conventional battery enclosures, offering bigger plates, more acid and extra starting power.

After decades of innovations, milestones, various marketing promotions and appearances in pop culture, including Batman comics, the Carol Burnett Show, *Days of Thunder* and keeping Johnny Five recharged in *Short Circuit 2*, the legendary battery finally teamed up with John McClane.

In October 2020, Advance Auto Parts launched the "DieHard is Back" campaign with a two-minute action-packed film featuring John McClane fighting off henchman, but this time his sidekick is a DieHard Platinum AGM battery. This ad also featured De'voreaux White (Argyle) and Clarence Gilyard Jr. (Theo).

Developed by George Marsaglia and first published on a CD-ROM in 1995, the diehard tests are a battery of statistical tests for measuring the quality of a random number generator.

In mathematician John Horton Conway's 1970 cellular automatic *Game of Life* (also known as *Life)* Diehard is a type of pattern that eventually disappears, rather than stabilizing, after 130 generations, which is conjectured to be maximal for patterns with seven or fewer cells.

The Talladega DieHard 500 is the former name for a NASCAR Cup Series stock car race held at Talladega Superspeedway in Lincoln, Alabama.

"Die Hard" has been used in song titles by musicians such as Kendrick Lamar, Venom, and Dr. Dre.

It's obvious that the phrase, like the movie, and like the battery, is one with a substantially long life.

IT'S NOT CHRISTMAS UNTIL HANS GRUBER FALLS OFF NAKATOMI TOWER

It is *too* a motherfucking Christmas movie!

Despite what Bruce Willis said in 1988 at his Comedy Central roast, the fun-filled debates about the movie's status as a Christmas classic rage on. That's because it's not only an annual seasonal tradition for so many to watch *Die Hard* along with other perennial classics, but it has become a custom to discuss the film's merits in that holiday genre.

> *"Die Hard is not a Christmas movie! It's a god damn Bruce Willis movie!"*
> —Bruce Willis, 1988

Because this was stated at a roast for Bruce Willis, and the way he jokingly called it a movie about himself, it's possible the actor wasn't sincere in this belief.

But there doesn't appear to be any follow-up on his re-stating or denying that claim.

Some entertainment pundits pointed out that Willis likes to troll the media and might have been trying to work people up into a frenzy.

Die Hard Cinematographer Jan de Bont seems to also be in the same camp regarding the movie's Christmas status. In a December 16, 2022, interview with *Yahoo* he told Ethan Alter he wasn't sure if the spirit of Christmas was fully embraced, and that to call the film a Christmas movie was "a little far-fetched."

While we do have evidence that a couple of people who worked on the film have publicly shared their views against it being a Christmas movie, let's look at what many others involved in the film say, and explore the reasons why *Die Hard* is considered a Christmas movie.

Script writer Steven E. de Souza is adamant in his belief that it is most definitely a Christmas film, saying that if *Die Hard* is not a Christmas movie, then neither is *White Christmas*.

At the time of the writing of this book De Souza's Twitter account features a July

29, 2022, pinned tweet that shares a graphic he created with the text: "This handy chart makes it clear!"

CHRISTMAS MOVIE OR NOT CHECK LIST

	DIE HARD	WHITE CHRISTMAS
Takes place during Christmas Holiday	Entirely	First and final scenes only
Setting a Christmas party	Entirely	Final scene only
Number of Christmas songs	Four ("Let it Snow," "Winter Wonderland," "Christmas in Hollis," "Jingle Bells")	Two ("White Christmas," "Snow")
Party venue threatened	By terrorists	By foreclosure
Broadcaster w/ Hidden Agenda	Dick Thornburg	Johnny Grant
German Ringleader	Hans Gruber	Hitler
Government Incompetence	FBI overreacts	Pentagon fires General Waverley
Body Count	23	26,128 (Battle of the Bulge opening scene)
"Gift of the Magi"-like selfless sacrifice	Running barefoot over broken glass	Danny Kaye upgrades Vera Ellen's train ticket

YOU BE THE JUDGE

Checklist comparing Die Hard to White Christmas from Steven E. de Souza's Twitter account: https://twitter.com/StevenEdeSouza

In a July 19, 2018, *Final Draft* interview with Anna Klassen, de Souza also asked who we are going to believe: An actor, the screenwriters, or 20th Century Fox?

He was referring to the fact that 20th Century Fox not only authorized the 2017 *Die Hard* and *The Night Before Christmas* mashup written by Doogie Horner, but they also formally admitted the film is a Christmas movie. They stated that, "it's the greatest Christmas story ever told," in a 2018 trailer to mark the 30th anniversary of the film's release.

Besides comparisons to *White Christmas*, there are other seasonal movies one might also consider.

For example, there are numerous parallels between John Hughes' Christmas perennial *Home Alone* and *Die Hard*. Both are about a single "warrior" trapped and alone in a building and using their wiles, found "weapons" and operating with a brutal efficiency to out-smart and out-last the infiltrating bad guys.

In fact, the author of *A Die Hard Christmas*, Doogie Horner, also created a mash-up of the two stories called *Home Alone Hard* which is available for free in eBook and Audiobook formats on his website.

Steven E. de Souza isn't the only one who is in that camp. Producer Joel Silver saw the movie's value as a Christmas movie. In a July 2018 *Washington Post* article by Alex Horton, de Souza said he witnessed the producer declaring that it would roar into syndication and be played on television at Christmastime for years.

The very set and design and look of the film is filled with colorful festive-inspired gold, green, and red set pieces and costumes. It might be stretching it, but even John McClane's white undershirt, marked with blood, creates a Santa-like red and white combination.

The movie's soundtrack not only includes Christmas songs and is scored with elements of "Jingle Bells" and "Ode to Joy" (a Beethoven classic strongly associated with Christmas) but both McClane and Powell can be heard muttering, singing, or whistling Christmas songs. (McClane whistles "Jingle Bells" when first walking to the elevators in the Nakatomi lobby, and Powell sings "Let It Snow" under his breath while purchasing Twinkies).

Here are some additional elements that lend to the film's status as a Christmas movie:

- It takes place on Christmas Eve and includes a figure one might consider "Santa-like" in that he sneaks around, mostly from above and mostly unseen. Not only that but there are people who believe in him and others who do not.

- The "Hallmark Christmas" movie trope of a protagonist getting "trapped" in a location. Plus, the additional element of travel to an environment associated with a former love interest.

- The events take place at a Christmas party, complete with Christmas tree and an orchestra playing Christmas music.

- Holly tells her assistant that she feels like "Ebenezer Scrooge" and, when speaking to her daughter about whether Daddy will come home with her she says: "We'll see what Mommy and Santa can do."

- McClane dresses dead terrorist Tony in a Santa hat and scrawls: "Now I have a machine gun. Ho – Ho – Ho" on his shirt.

- Hans and Theo make numerous references to Christmas such as it being the time of miracles, to "be of good cheer" and "The Night Before Christmas."

- When the vault finally opens, and "Ode to Joy" plays, Theo and Hans stand in awe as they are bathed in a white light, reacting almost as if they are witnessing the star of Bethlehem.

- McClane secures a hidden handgun to the back of his shoulders with festive Christmas tape.

- It snows at the end. Sure, the "snow" happens to be thousands of reams of paper, mostly the bearer bonds, but it does lend to that "miracle" end of a snow in LA, a "white Christmas" after all.

Regardless of where you stand on the matter, the debate on whether it's a Christmas movie or not among fans continues to this day and in numerous environments.

A company that I work part-time for even has a question built-in to their interview process that is meant to explore an applicant's creativity. They ask "Is *Die Hard* a Christmas movie? Explain why or why not?" This company—*Draft2Digital,* a provider of free tools to help writers interested in DIY publishing—has traditionally included a home-made decoration featuring John McClane crawling through the air vent on the Christmas tree in their Oklahoma City based head office. And the company's Slack channel is rife with *Die Hard* references and memes alluding to the fact that most people who work there are adamant in their belief of the movie's standing as a Christmas classic.

But the debate, and passionate discussion, continue. Why? Perhaps because it's just plain fun.

It might also be because, like the timeless classic that we love, it's one of those conflicts we simply enjoy returning to time and again.

Image adapted from:
Alan Rickman, Die Hard (20th Century Fox, 1988)

AJ Pics / Alamy Stock Photo

Don't forget to leave cigarettes, shoes, and Twinkies in the ductwork for John McClane on Christmas Eve

Image adapted from:
Bruce Willis, Die Hard (20th Century Fox, 1988)

Atlaspix / Alamy Stock Photo

HOW COULD THE SAME SHIT HAPPEN TO THE SAME GUY ~~TWICE~~...FIVE TIMES?

A crawl through the *Die Hard* franchise

Yes, this book is focused on *Die Hard*. But we can't really talk about the movie without exploring the further adventures of John McClane.

Following is a high-level look at the other films in the franchise with a handful of trivial tidbits and anecdotes about each.

DIE HARD 2: DIE HARDER

Die Hard 2: Die Harder released on July 4, 1990, earning $21.7 million on its first weekend, grossing $46 million by the end of the first week, $118 million in the US and $122 million internationally.

• More gags were added to the sequel, and Willis was invited to do more ad lib one-liners as John McClane

• When producer Joel Silver read the initial script, he kept thinking "How can the same thing happen to the same guy twice?" That was incorporated into the meta-style reflections of John McClane in the film for humor. This similar self-reflection occurs when Major Grant says he is the "wrong guy in the wrong place at the wrong time" and McClane responds: "Yeah, story of my life."

• The scene where John McClane climbs the ladder from the service tunnels below the airport runways and nearly gets run over by Esperanza's plan was filmed from six different locations:
  ○ Granada Hills, CA—in tunnel and climbing ladder
  ○ Los Angeles, CA—Close-ups inside plane's cockpit
  ○ Mojave Desert, CA—Head-on view of plane on approach
  ○ Alpena, MI—Exterior shot of grating on runway

- o San Francisco, CA—Rear shot of plane on approach to runway
- o Sault Ste. Marie, MI—Plane after landing rushing towards the screen
- o Denver, CO—View from behind landing gear as plane rushes at McClane

- When airport manager Ed Trudeau says that they only have 58 minutes to avoid disaster, it's a reference to the novel *58 Minutes* by Walter Wager which served as inspiration for the screenplay.

- In one of the dubs to remove the foul language, McClane's famous line "Yippee-ki-yay motherfucker" was dubbed into "Yippee-ki-yay Mr. Falcon." Esperanza's codename in the movie is Falcon.

DIE HARD WITH A VENGEANCE

This third film in the franchise—the first not to be set at Christmas—opened in the United States on May 19, 1995, and earned $22.2 million on its opening weekend, ranking in first place at the box office, beating out Crimson Tide. It grossed $100 million in the United States and Canada, and more than two hundred and sixty-six million dollars in other markets, giving it a total worldwide gross of more than $366 million, making it the highest-grossing film of 1995.

• There were two alternative endings to the film. One, found on the Special Feature DVD, presumes the robbery was successful and McClane later tracks Simon down and plays a game he calls "McClane Says" and he brutally enacts his vengeance. This ending was scrapped because of its portrayal of McClane as cruel and killing for revenge rather than self-defense.

• The movie's release was almost delayed due to the tragic events of the Oklahoma City bombing in April of the same year. During a press conference promoting the film's release, Bruce Willis pre-emptively told reporters he would not discuss that bombing as he didn't want to trivialize that real-world tragedy by comparing it in any way to a fictional movie.

• In the movie Simon forces John McClane to wear a sandwich board that reads "I hate [*plural of the n-word*]" in the middle of Harlem. For the filming, the sign read "I hate everybody" and was changed using CGI effects in post-production.

• This is the first of the movie franchises to be set in the city where John McClane works as a cop. The previous two were set in Los Angeles, CA, and in Dulles, VA.

• Although he wasn't hired to be in the film Alan Rickman's name appears in the credits as Hans Gruber, Simon's brother, who is seen in McClane's flashback to the events from the first film in the franchise.

LIVE FREE OR DIE HARD

Live Free or Die Hard was released in the US on June 27, 2007, and debuted in second place at the box office behind *Ratatouille*. It made $9.1 million in its first day and on its opening weekend (including the Wed and Thurs) it earned $48.3 million. The film made $134.5 million domestically, $249 million overseas for a total of $383.5 million, making it the twelfth highest-grossing film of 2007.

• The televised warning from Gabriel combining archive footage of past American presidents from Franklin D. Roosevelt to George W. Bush—a video representation of a ransom note—took four months to assemble.

• Justin Long, who plays hacker Matthew "Matt" Farrell, was known for appearing as a "Mac" in Apple's 2006 "Get a Mac" television adverting campaign.

• The film earned $9.1 million in its first day of release in 3,172 theaters, seeing the best opening day take of any film in the *Die Hard* series (not counting for inflation).

• Stuntman (and double for Bruce Willis) Larry Rippenkroeger was seriously injured—suffering fractures in both wrists and broken bones in his face—when he fell twenty-five feet to the pavement. Willis visited him in the hospital and picked up the tab when the stuntman's family visited from out of town.

A GOOD DAY TO DIE HARD

A Good Day to Die Hard premiered on January 31, 2013, grossing $67.3 million in North America and $237.3 million elsewhere, resulting in a worldwide total of $304.7 million.

• The January 31, 2013, premiere of the movie coincided with a special 25th anniversary tribute to the franchise. 20th Century Fox unveiled a mural of a scene with John McClane crawling through the air vents in *Die Hard* on Sound Stage 8 of the Fox Lot. After, the premiere screening of *A Good Day to Die Hard* was shown, and a party was held on the 21st Floor of Fox Plaza. (No robbers posing as terrorists interrupted that particular party).

• The script for this film was the first in the franchise to not be based on other source material. The original screenplay was written specifically as an entry in the *Die Hard* series. It was also panned by critics and ranks the lowest among many fans. Evidence that, like a fine wine or whiskey, a good script might need to "age?" You be the judge.

• The ringtone on John McClane's phone is Beethoven's "Ode to Joy"—a nod to the "Hans Gruber theme" from the first film.

• The movie poster for the film used the phrase "Yippee Ki Yay Mother Russia."

DIEHARD IS BACK

In October of 2020 Advance Auto Parts created a two-minute commercial that acts as a mini sequel and is considered by many fans to be the unofficial "sixth film" in the franchise.

Bruce Willis appears in what would mark his final appearance as John McClane (the actor announced his retirement from acting in 2022, and has been diagnosed with having aphasia and frontotemporal dementia). De'voreaux White returns as limousine driver Argyle. And Clarence Gilyard reprises his role as Theo.

In the ad, John McClane's car battery dies while he is driving at night down an empty street adjacent to a construction site. He leaves his car to walk to a nearby Advance Auto Parts store when he runs into Theo who acts as the leader of a group of fresh thugs.

McClane dodges their gunfire and crashes through the store's front window then quickly buys a battery from the clerk. When he asks if there's another way out, she points to the air vent in the ceiling.

After looking up at the vent, then back at her and saying: "Are you kidding me?" McClane crawls through the air duct and makes his way outside.

While running along the street he is struck by a car and is surprised to see Argyle is the driver. Argyle gives him a lift, swerving to avoid the flying bullets and complains about McClane getting blood on the seat and the fact that he'd just paid this car off.

One of the thugs rams the limo with a Humvee, knocking out Argyle. McClane drags his friend and the battery back to his car.

When more bad guys arrive, McClane slams one of them with the battery. The DieHard is hit by a bullet, but he continues to install it—demonstrating his faith in the brand. Argyle, finally coming to, starts the car.

Theo then arrives in a backhoe. McClane throws a grenade into the cockpit, yelling out "Happy trails!" before getting in the passenger seat, but Theo doesn't notice.

Argyle then drives away with Theo chasing them in the backhoe. After a few tense moments, the grenade explodes, killing Theo and destroying the backhoe.

• The female clerk in the store can be heard humming "Ode to Joy" under her breath before McClane comes crashing through the front window. The same theme is incorporated into the short's climactic finish.

• Neither Theo nor Argyle had been seen since the 1998 original film in the franchise.

- The short film was written by Nick Cernoch and Harris Wilson and was directed by John Suit.

A few other *Die Hard* related movies and television programs were in the works, but as of the release of this book in July 2023, none of them have yet seen the light of day.

- In 2013, Fox Studios began looking a developing the next installment and started taking pitches for a project they were tentatively titling "Die Hardest."

- That same year rumors were floating around about a script entitled *Old Habits Die Hard*.

- A crossover with the popular television program, *24* featuring characters from the *Die Hard* franchise had been considered, but contract negotiations with Kiefer Sutherland went sour and no pilot was ever made.

• In 2015 *Live Free or Die Hard* the pre-quel/sequel written by director Len Wiseman called "John McClane" began to gain a bit of traction but ended up stalling.

•In the summer of 2017 Weiseman was in negotiations to direct a stand-alone mini-series of twelve episodes of a show called *Die Hard: Year One* based on the BOOM! Studios graphic novel of the same name. It would be narrated by the voice of Bruce Willis as a flash-back look at McClane's first year as a rookie cop. Wiseman began to look at casting for the role of the young John McClane.

• In July of 2018 producer Lorenzo di Bonaventura called for an updated treat-ment of the script titled *McClane*. Rumors were floating around of an interest in cast-ing *Teen Wolf* star Dylan O'Brien in the role of the young John McClane. But the acquisition of 20th Century Fox by Disney resulted in a production hiatus in the summer of 2019. And by the summer of 2021 di Bonaventura officially announced the project was a "no-go."

• And while it's not a part of the franchise, there is a short video of Bruce Willis looking reflective while standing atop the building of "Nakatomi Plaza" in July of 2022 for the 34th Anniversary of the release. It was recorded and shared by Emma Heming Willis (wife of Bruce Willis) on her Instagram account. A black and white short clip of the actor leaning on a railing and looking out across the city, is followed by iconic scenes from the classic film, and is perhaps the perfect way for John McClane, and actor Bruce Willis, to enjoy a fitting, and touching sunset.

YIPPEE KI-YAY

And other memorable one-liners, quips,
and catch phrases from the film

There is no discounting the fact that "Yippee Ki-Yay Motherfucker!" is one of those most recognizable lines that transcends the film. That is, after all, one of the reasons I chose it for the title of this book.

In 2016 the line was listed #26 by *The Hollywood Reporter* readers voting on the most memorable quote from any movie ever made. The line was ranked #96 of "The 100 Greatest Movie Lines" by Premiere magazine in 2007. And in that same year *Slate* magazine called it the greatest one-liner in movie history.

The phrase was used in all of the films in the franchise. Here are the scenarios for the line's use in each film.

- *Die Hard*: Talking on the radio with Hans Gruber McClane utters the line in response to being asked if he thinks he really stands a chance. Later in the film, Hans uses the line mockingly as he raises his gun to shoot McClane.

- *Die Hard 2: Die Harder*: Prior to being pushed off the wing of the plane by Colonel Stuart as it races down the runway, McClane removes the cap from the fuel tank. Just as the plane is taking off, McClane throws his cigarette lighter, igniting the fuel trail and yelling the catch phrase just before the flame shoots up to the plane and it explodes.

- *Die Hard with a Vengeance*: After shooting at power lines which fall and get tangled in the rotors of the helicopter causing it to crash and killing Simon Gruber, McClane utters the words under his breath. (In the original script—and in the novelization of the film—McClane says the line to Gruber over the CB when in the aqueduct. The film producers changed it to happen in the climax to match *Die Hard 2*.

- *Live Free or Die Hard*: As Gabriel holds McClane from behind, with his gun pressed against McClane's gunshot shoulder, he suggests that his tombstone should read: "Always in the wrong place at the wrong time!" Grabbing the gun and shooting Gabriel in the chest through his own shoulder, McClane replies: "How about 'Yippee-Ki-Kay, motherfucker?" (The "motherfucker" part of the line was obscured by the gunshot to ensure the film maintained its PG-13 rating. The line was restored later in the unrated version)

- *A Good Day to Die Hard*: As McClane manages to jump onto the back of Irina's helicopter and get into the dump truck located in the copter's cargo hold he engages the engine and says: "The shit we do for our kids! Yippee-Ki-Yay motherfucker!" (Many critics and fans alike complained that the line was "wasted" and used in the film at a non-dramatic moment. Previously it had been used for comedic ironic purposes in taunting the antagonist or when the film's villain was killed)

- *DieHard is Back*: (Two-minute short film commercial by Advance Auto Parts promoting the DieHard battery brand). As Theo is left to die in an explosion, Argyle begins uttering the catchphrase, but McClane cuts him off, saying: "Hey! That's my line!"

Yes, John. It *is* your line. And always will be. But before it became something you added a whole new meaning to, it had a unique and interesting origin story.

First, let's look at the spelling, and the variations that appear in the script and in writings about the film.

The phrase itself is spelled in numerous ways. The most popular versions are:

Yippie-ki-yay.
Yippee-ki-yay.
Yippee-ki-yea.

The hyphen appearing between the words in the phrase is often optional.

In the script for the film, it's spelled out two different ways. The first time it is used, when McClane utters it, the script reads:

Yipee-yi-yea

Later in the movie, when Hans mockingly quotes McClane, it is spelled:

Yippe-ki-yea

Oxford English Reference Dictionary spells the word *yippee* and defines it as "expressing delight or excitement." That's one of the reasons I opted to go with that spelling for the title of this book.

But let's first take a look at the origin of phrase, before John McClane tacked on the unforgettable "motherfucker" to the end of it.

Yippee is derived from the word term *yip* which originated as *yippen* in the 15th Century Middle English, then later shortened to *yip* in the 19th Century and meant "to cheep, as a young bird" (Oxford) or a "short, sharp cry" (Cambridge). *Yippee* as an exclamation of delight appeared in print in 1920 in the novel **Main Street** by Sinclair Lewis.

She galloped down a block and as she jumped from a curb across a welter of slush, she gave a student 'Yippee!'

The phrase *yippee-ki-yay* is possibly derived from the refrain "yippee yi yo kayah" in the 1930 Bing Crosby song (written by Johnny Mercer) "I'm an Old Cowhand."

Roy Rogers later popularized the phrase in his 1943 version of the song and then in the 1950s on *The Roy Rogers Show* when he would utter "yippee-ki-yah, kids!"

But since 1988 when John McClane first uttered it to Hans Gruber over the radio, it has remained a phrase tied to him.

Apart from this highly referenced one-liner that has expanded well beyond the franchise, *Die Hard* is filled with many other quotable lines, quips, and moments.

Following are additional memorable lines and one-liners from the film, identifying who said them, the actor playing that role, and whether the line was scripted or an ad lib.

"I was hoping you could tell me. This is my first day driving a limo." [*Responding to McClane asking "What do we do now?"*]
—Argyle (De'voreaux White)

"That's okay, it's my first time riding in one."
—John McClane (Bruce Willis)

"In other words, you thought she wasn't going to make it out here, and she'd come crawling back to you. So why bother to pack, right?"
—Argyle (De'voreaux White)

"This *is* Christmas music." [*playing Run DMC's 'Christmas in Hollis'*]
—Argyle (De'voreaux White)

"Yeah, if you have to take a leak it'll even help you find your zipper." [*In response to John's comment "Cute toy" about the computer directory*]
—Guard (Rick Cicetti)

"Jesus. Fucking California" [*after being kissed on the cheek by a stranger at the Christmas party*]
—John McClane (Bruce Willis)

"You missed some." [*To Ellis, in reference to the cocaine residue still visible on his nose*]
—John McClane (Bruce Willis)

"Hey, we're flexible. Pearl Harbor didn't work out, so we got you with tape decks." [*In response to McClane saying he didn't realize they celebrated Christmas in Japan*]
—Joseph Takagi (James Shigeta)

"That's okay. I have my eye on his private bathroom." [*In response to McClane saying that Ellis has his eyes on her*]
—Holly Gennaro (Bonnie Bedelia)

"Son of a bitch. Fists with your toes."
—John McClane (Bruce Willis)

"Ladies and gentlemen. Due to the Nakatomi Corporation's legacy of greed around the globe, they are about to be taught a lesson in the real use of power. You will be witnesses."
— Hans Gruber (Alan Rickman)

"Nice Suit. John Phillips, London. I have two myself. Rumor has it Arafat buys his there."
—Hans Gruber (Alan Rickman)

"'And when Alexander saw the breadth of his domain, he wept, for there were no more worlds to conquer.' Benefits of a classical education."

—Hans Gruber (Alan Rickman)

"Mr. Takagi, I could talk about industrialization and men's fashions all day, but I'm afraid work must intrude, and my associate, Theo, has some questions for you. Sort of *fill in the blanks* questions, actually."
—Hans Gruber (Alan Rickman)

"That's a very nice suit, Mr. Takagi. It would be a shame to ruin it. I'm going to count to three. There will not be a four. Give me the code."
—Hans Gruber (Alan Rickman)

"You didn't bring me along for my charming personality."
—Theo (Clarence Gilyard Jr.)

"C'mon baby, come ta' papa, I'll kiss your fuckin' dalmatian!"
—John McClane (Bruce Willis)

"The fire has been called off, my friend. No one is coming to help you. You might as well come out and join the others. [*locking and loading his gun*] I promise I won't hurt you."
—Tony Vreski (Andreas Wisniewski)

"Yeah, that's what my captain keeps tell me."
[*in response to Tony saying he wasn't in risk of being hurt because there are rules for policemen*]
—John McClane (Bruce Willis)

"Nine million terrorists in the world and I gotta kill one with feet smaller than my sister."
—John McClane (Bruce Willis)

"I wanted this to be professional, efficient, adult, cooperative. Not a lot to ask. Alas, your Mr. Takagi did not see it that way . . . so he won't be joining us for the rest of his life."
—Hans Gruber (Alan Rickman)

[*Reading what McClane wrote on the dead terrorist's sweater*] "Now I have a machine gun. Ho . . . ho . . . ho."
—Hans Gruber (Alan Rickman)

"No fucking shit, lady. Do I sound like I'm ordering a pizza?"
— John McClane (Bruce Willis)

"Thought you guys just ate donuts."
— Convenience Store Clerk (Kip Waldo)

"Come out to the coast, we'll get together, have a few laughs."
— John McClane (Bruce Willis)

"Now I know what a TV dinner feels like."
— John McClane (Bruce Willis) – ad lib

"Who's driving this car, Stevie Wonder?"
— John McClane (Bruce Willis)

"Welcome to the party, pal!"
— John McClane (Bruce Willis)

"I'm in Nakatomi Plaza. They're turning my car into Swiss cheese! I need backup assistance now! NOW, GODDAMMIT, NOW!"
—Sergeant Al Powell (Reginald VelJohnson)

"Eeeh! Sorry Hans, wrong guess. Would you like to go for Double Jeopardy where the scores can really change?"
—John McClane (Bruce Willis)

"Ohh, these are very bad for you." [*Pulling a pack of cigarettes out of a dead terrorist's pocket*]
—John McClane (Bruce Willis)

"Just a fly in the ointment, Hans. A monkey in the wrench. A pain in the ass."
—John McClane (Bruce Willis)

"You know my name, but who are you? Just another American who saw too many movies as a child? Another orphan of a bankrupt culture who thinks he's John Wayne? Rambo? Marshall Dillon?"
— Hans Gruber (Alan Rickman)

"I was always kinda partial to Roy Rogers, actually. I really like those sequined shirts."
— John McClane (Bruce Willis)

"Do you really think you have a chance against us, Mr. Cowboy?"
— Hans Gruber (Alan Rickman)

"Yippee Ki-Yay, motherfucker!"
—John McClane (Bruce Willis)

"Listen fast. It's a party line and the neighbors got itchy trigger fingers."
—John McClane (Bruce Willis)

"They've got missiles, automatic weapons, and enough plastique explosives to orbit Arnold Schwarzenegger."
—John McClane (Bruce Willis)

"I've seen enough phony IDs in my time to recognize that the ones they got must have cost a fortune. Add all that up, I don't know what the fuck it means, but you got some bad-ass perpetrators and they're here to stay."
— John McClane (Bruce Willis)

"I hear you, partner. LA's finest are on it. So light 'em if you got 'em."
—Sergeant Al Powell (Reginald VelJohnson)

"Call me . . . Roy."
— John McClane (Bruce Willis)

"Jesus Christ, Powell, he could be a fucking bartender for all we know."
—Deputy Chief Dwayne T. Robinson (Paul Gleason)

"What idiot put you in charge?"
—Hans Gruber (Alan Rickman)

"You did. When you murdered my boss. Now everybody's looking to me. Personally,

I'd pass on the job. I don't enjoy being this close to you."
— Holly Gennaro (Bonnie Bedelia)

"And unless you like it messy, I'd start bringing us in groups to the bathroom."
— Holly Gennaro (Bonnie Bedelia)

"If you are what I think you are then you'll know when to shut up, when to listen . . . and when to pray."
— Sergeant Al Powell (Reginald VelJohnson)

"Shut up!" [*to the teddy bear in the back of his limo*]
— Argyle (De'voreaux White)

"All right, listen up guys. 'Twas the night before Christmas, and all through the house, not a creature was stirring . . . except the four assholes coming in the rear in a standard two-by-two cover formation."
— Theo (Clarence Gilyard Jr.)

"Woah. Wait a minute, wait a minute. What have we here, gentlemen? The police have themselves an RV."
— Theo (Clarence Gilyard Jr.)

"Oh my god! The quarterback *is* toast!"
—Theo (Clarence Gilyard Jr.) - ad lib

"Geronimo, motherfucker."
— John McClane (Bruce Willis)

"Eat your heart out, Channel 5."
— Richard Thornburg (William Atherton)

"No, but it's gonna need a paint job and a shit load of screen doors." [*In response to being asked by McClane if the building is on fire*]
—Sergeant Al Powell (Reginald VelJohnson)

"Oh, *you're* in charge? Well, I've got some bad news for you, *Dwayne*—from up here it doesn't look like you're in charge of jack shit."
—John McClane (Bruce Willis)

"Asshole? I'm not the one who just got butt-fucked on national TV, *Dwayne*. Now, you listen to me, jerk-off, if you're not a part of the solution, you're a part of the problem. Quit being a part of the fucking problem and put the other guy back on!"
—John McClane (Bruce Willis)

"Hey, babe. I negotiate million-dollar deals for breakfast. I think I can handle this Eurotrash."
—Harry Ellis (Hart Bochner)

"Hey, business is business. You use a gun; I use a fountain pen. What's the difference? Let's put it in my terms: you're here on a hostile takeover, you grab us up for some green mail, but you're not expecting some poison pill was going to be running around the building, am I right?"
—Ellis (Hart Bochner)

"Hans, bubby, I'm your white knight."
—Ellis (Hart Bochner) – ad lib

"I must have missed 60 Minutes. What are you saying?"
—Hans Gruber (Alan Rickman)

"Sister Teresa called me Mr. McClane in the third grade. My friends call me John, and you're neither, shit-head."
— John McClane (Bruce Willis)

"The man is hurting! He is alone, tired, and he hasn't seen diddly-squat from anybody down here. Now you're gonna stand there and tell me that he's gonna give a damn about what

you do to him, *if* he makes it out of there alive? Why don't you wake up and smell what you shoveling?"
—Sergeant Al Powell (Reginald VelJohnson)

"It's Christmas, Theo. It's the time of miracles. So be of good cheer . . . and call me when you hit the last lock."
—Hans Gruber (Alan Rickman)

"Hey, don't ask me, man. I'm just a desk jockey who was on my way home when you rang."
—Sergeant Al Powell (Reginald VelJohnson)

"Want a breath mint?" [*To Dept. Robinson who starts to straight his suit and tie when he hears the FBI have arrived*]
—Sergeant Al Powell (Reginald VelJohnson)

"I'm Agent Johnson. This is Special Agent Johnson. . . . No relation."
—FBI Agent Johnson (Grand L. Bush)

"Thank you. We'll handle it from here. When we commander your men we'll try and let you know."
—FBI Agent Johnson (Grand L. Bush)

"I got invited to the Christmas party by mistake. Who knew?"
— John McClane (Bruce Willis)

"It's better than being caught with your pants down, you know?" [*To Gruber who notices his bare feet*]
— John McClane (Bruce Willis)

"That's pretty tricky with that accent. You oughta be on fucking TV with that accent. But what do you want with the detonators, Hans? I already used all the explosives. Or did I?"
— John McClane (Bruce Willis)

"Karl, Schieß dem Fenster. Shoot the glass!"
—Hans Gruber (Alan Rickman)

"He's still alive. . . . only John can drive somebody that crazy."
—Holly Gennaro (Bonnie Bedelia)

"Yeah. But all things being equal, I'd rather be in Philadelphia. Chalk up two more bad guys."
— John McClane (Bruce Willis)

"You know when you're a rookie they can teach you everything about being a cop, except how to live with a mistake."
—Sergeant Al Powell (Reginald VelJohnson)

"The circuits that cannot be cut are cut automatically in response to a terrorist incident. You asked for miracles, Theo, I give you the F.B.I."
— Hans Gruber (Alan Rickman)

"Authorization? How about the United States *fucking* government? Lose the grid, or you lose your job."
—FBI Special Agent Johnson (Robert Davi)

"Yeah Central? Yeah, this is Walt down at Nakatomi. Uh, say, listen, uh, would it be possible for you to turn off Grid 212?"
—Walt (Rick Ducommun)

"Well, what are we gonna do now? Arrest them for not paying their electric bill?"
—Sergeant Al Powell (Reginald VelJohnson)

"Those bastards are probably pissing their pants right now."
—FBI Special Agent Johnson (Robert Davi)

"This is agent Johnson. No, the other one."
—FBI Special Agent Johnson (Robert Davi)

"When they touch down, we'll blow the roof, they'll spend a month sifting through rubble, and by the time they figure out what went wrong, we'll be sitting on a beach, earning twenty percent."
— Hans Gruber (Alan Rickman)

"I want you to find my wife. Don't ask me how; by then you'll know how. I want you to tell her something . . . I want you to tell her that . . . tell her that it took me a while to figure out what a jerk I've been. But, uhm, that . . . that when things started to pan out for her, I shoulda . . . been more supportive. And, uh, I just shoulda been behind her more. Oh shit. Tell her that . . . she's the best thing that ever happen to a bum like me. She's heard me say 'I love you' a thousand times. But she's never heard me say 'I'm sorry.' Now I want you to tell her that, Al. I want you to tell her that, ah . . . John said . . . that he was sorry. Okay? You got that, man?"
— John McClane (Bruce Willis)

"Mrs. McClane. How nice to make your acquaintance."
— Hans Gruber (Alan Rickman)

"You shoulda heard your brother squeal . . . when I broke his fucking neck."
— John McClane (Bruce Willis)

"After all your posturing, all your little speeches, you're nothing but a common thief."
—Holly Gennaro (Bonnie Bedelia)

"I am an exceptional thief, Mrs. McClane. And since I'm moving up to kidnapping, you should be more polite."
— Hans Gruber (Alan Rickman)

"Mother fucker, I'm gonna kill you. I'm gonna fucking cook ya. I'm gonna fucking eat you."
— John McClane (Bruce Willis)

"I promise I will never even *think* about going up in a tall building again." [*As he is about to jump off the top of the building with a firehose tied around his waist*]
— John McClane (Bruce Willis)

"We're gonna need some new FBI guys, I guess."
—Deputy Chief Dwayne T. Robinson (Paul Gleason)

"Hi, honey."
— John McClane (Bruce Willis) - ad lib

"Why'd you have to nuke the whole building, Hans?"
— John McClane (Bruce Willis)

"When you steal $600, you can just disappear. When you steal 600 million, they will find you, unless they think you're already dead."
— Hans Gruber (Alan Rickman)

"Still the cowboy, Mr. McClane. Americans, all alike. Well, this time John Wayne does not walk off into the sunset with Grace Kelly."
— Hans Gruber (Alan Rickman)

"That's Gary Cooper, asshole."
— John McClane (Bruce Willis)

"Happy trails, Hans!"
— John McClane (Bruce Willis)

"Oh, I hope that's not a hostage."
—Deputy Chief Dwayne T. Robinson (Paul Gleason)

"Did you get *that*?"
— Richard Thornburg (William Atherton) – ad lib

"If this is their idea of Christmas, I gotta be here for New Year's."
—Argyle (De'voreaux White)

DUM DE DUM DELIGHTFUL
The sound track

The movie contains an original score composed by Michael Kamen (April 15, 1948—November 18, 2003), who won a BMI/Film Music Award for his work. Kamen also won BMI awards for his work on *Die Hard 2: Die Harder, Die Hard with a Vengeance,* the four *Lethal Weapon* films, *Robin Hood: Prince of Thieves, X-Men, Band of Brothers, Mr. Holland's Opus,* and many more. His work on *Die Hard* not only won him an award, but received critical acclaim among reviewers from *Movie Wave, Mfiles, Allmusic,* and *Filmtracks.com.*

In addition to the score, the movie also contains several diegetic music pieces. Diegetic music, also known as source music, is when music appears within the fictional setting of a drama and is knowingly performed and heard by the characters. Some examples of this would be the orchestra that is playing in the lobby of the

Nakatomi Christmas party, the music heard on the stereo in the limousine, John McClane whistling "Jingle Bells" when he's walking through the front lobby on his way to the Christmas party, or Al Powell muttering the words to "Let it Snow" under his breath when walking back to his police cruiser.

Director John McTiernan wanted to include *Beethoven's 9th Symphony* (also commonly known as "Ode to Joy" – a name he admitted he'd forgotten until after he had already locked onto his desire to use it) as an underlying bit of music throughout the film. Initially, Michael Kamen was opposed to the idea, objecting to the idea of "tarnishing" the classic in an action film. But Kamen better understood the director's intentions after McTiernan explained he was fascinated with the way it was used in the Kubrick film *A Clockwork Orange* to highlight the ultra-violence.

Kamen mixed in elements of "Ode to Joy" throughout the score for the film. (He also did this with the Christmas songs "Winter Wonderland" and "Let it Snow" as well as "Singin' in the Rain" (which was also used in *A Clockwork Orange*.

Beethoven's song can also be heard in that aforementioned diegetic way when Theo is humming the tune while hacking into the building's computers, ripping out wires, and kicking at computer panels near the beginning of the film. Hans Gruber also vocalizes the beats to the song in the elevator on the way to the Nakato-mi board room just before he compliments Mr. Takagi on his "nice suit." He hums it again as he is first entering the entrance to the board room.

It is reprised to ultimate dramatic effect in the scene immediately after the FBI shuts down power to the building which triggers the final lock and the vault opens as Hans, Theo and one other crew member stand in awe.

One of the major things that changed in the film's soundtrack was that Kamen had composed a score based on the continued use of "Ode to Joy" for the very final sequence as John and Holly get into the limo and drive off.

When editor Frank J. Urioste heard it, on the very last night before the deadline to get the video and audio mixed, he said that his heart sank in the way it ruined the ending of the movie. He immediately called Silver to review it, and the producer agreed. That Beethoven piece was tied to Gruber and his crew throughout the film, and just didn't work for the positive and "romantic" ending.

With McTiernan on vacation and unreachable, Urioste and Silver had to make a call on how to fix it, and so "mashed" together the temp music Kamen had originally provided along with bits.

And, despite the initial disagreement, it was clear that adding "Let it Snow!" to that ending sequence was the perfect "feel good" element that was needed.

The album for the soundtrack was not released with the movie in 1988. It was not released until almost 14 years later, in February 2002 courtesy of Varese Sarabande's CD club.

The original release contained only 21 tracks from the film's score all composed and performed by Michael Kamen.

2002 Release Track Listing

1. The Nakatomi Plaza - 01:50
2. Gruber's Arrival - 03:40
3. John's Escape/You Want Money? - 05:52
4. The Tower - 01:49
5. The Roof - 03:57
6. The Fight - 01:07
7. He Won't Be Joining Us - 03:53
8. And If He Alters It? - 02:39
9. Going After John Again - 04:33
10. Have a Few Laughs - 03:29
11. Welcome to the Party - 01:00
12. TV Station/His Bag Is Missing - 03:52
13. Assault on the Tower - 08:16
14. John Is Found Out - 05:03
15. Attention Police - 03:38
16. Bill Clay - 02:02
17. I Had an Accident - 02:37
18. Ode to Joy - 03:36
19. The Battle - 10:15
20. Gruber's Departure - 01:56
21. Let It Snow! Let It Snow! Let It Snow! - 02:00

The full score album was released in 2011 by La-La Land Records as part of a two-disc set that featured score cues and musical references heard in the movie. They re-issued it again in 2017.

2011 & 2017 Reissue Track Listing

Disc 1

1. Main Title (Mono Source) - 0:38
2. Terrorist Entrance - 4:05
3. The Phone Goes Dead / Party Crashers - 1:51
4. John's Escape / You Want Money - 6:00
5. Wiring the Roof - 1:51
6. Fire Alarm - 2:04
7. Tony Approaches - 1:41
8. Tony and John Fight - 1:11
9. Santa - 0:55
10. He Won't Be Joining Us - 3:01
11. And If He Alters It - 2:39
12. Going After John - 4:29
13. Have A Few Laughs / Al Powell Approaches - 3:31
14. Under the Table - 1:55
15. Welcome to the Party - 1:09
16. TV Station - 2:47
17. Holly Meets Hans - 1:19
18. Assault On the Tower - 8:35

Disc 2

19. John Is Found Out - 5:03
20. Attention Police - 3:54
21. Bill Clay - 4:09
22. Shooting the Glass - 1:05
23. I Had an Accident - 2:37
24. The Vault - 3:07
25. Message for Holly - 1:07
26. The Battle / Freeing the Hostages - 6:53
27. Helicopter Explosion and Showdown - 4:00

28. Happy Trails - 1:12
29. We've Got Each Other" (John Scott) - 1:56
30. Let It Snow" (Vaughn Monroe) - 1:43
31. Beethoven's 9th (End Credits Excerpt)" (Ludwig van Beethoven) - 3:54

Bonus tracks
32. The Nakatomi Plaza - 1:45
33. Message for Holly (Film Version, mono source) - 2:46
34. Gun in Cheek (mono source) - 1:01
35. Fire House (mono source) - 1:00
36. Ode to Joy (Alternate) - 2:10
37. Let It Snow (Source)" (Michael Kamen) 1:58
38. Winter Wonderland (Source) - 0:20
39. Christmas in Hollis" (Run-DMC) - 4:49

To coincide with the 30th anniversary of the movie La-La Land Records released a 3-disc-set remastered edition that included previously unreleased material from Kamen's original score, cues, pieces of diegetic music referenced in the film, source music, alternatives, and mixes heard in the movie.

30th Anniversary Remastered Edition

Disc 1
1. Main Title - 0:43
2. Seeing Holly - 1:07
3. Terrorist Entrance - 4:06

4. The Phone Goes Dead / Party Crashers - 1:53
5. John's Escape / You Want Money - 6:01
6. The Nakatomi Plaza (Takagi's Death) - 1:45
7. Wiring The Roof - 1:51
8. Approaching The Vault[P] - 0:48
9. Fire Alarm - 2:04
10. Tony Approaches - 1:42
11. Tony And John Fight - 1:13
12. Santa - 0:57
13. He Won't Be Joining Us - 3:02
14. And If He Alters It - 2:40
15. Going After John - 4:32
16. Have A Few Laughs / Al Powell Approaches - 3:32
17. Under The Table - 1:59
18. Welcome To The Party - 1:10
19. Yippee Ki-Yay[O] - 0:45
20. Holly Meets Hans - 1:20
21. Assault On The Tower - 8:34
22. John Is Found Out - 5:04
23. Attention Police - 3:54
24. Bill Clay - 4:09
25. Shoot The Glass[O] - 2:20
26. I Had An Accident (Extended Version)[O] - 2:56

Disc 2

27. The Vault (Film Edit) - 3:07
28. Message For Holly (Film Edit) [O] - 3:13
29. Gun In Cheek (Extended Version) [O] - 1:20
30. The Battle / Freeing The Hostages - 6:53
31. The Fire Hose[O] - 1:24
32. Helicopter Explosion And Showdown - 4:02
33. Happy Trails, Hans[P] - 1:42
34. Aftermath – Powell's Comeback[P] - 2:52

35. Let It Snow (Vaughn Monroe) - 1:44

36. Beethoven's 9th (End Credit Excerpt) - 3:53

37. Main Title (Alternate)[P] - 0:40

38. The Nakatomi Plaza (Takagi's Death) (Alternate)[P] - 1:47

39. Approaching The Vault (Alternates)[P] - 2:33

40. Tony Approaches (Alternate)[P] - 1:43

41. Yippee Ki-Yay (Extended Version) - 2:48

42. Assault On The Tower (Alternate Excerpts)[P] - 3:44

43. Attention Police (Pick Up Opening)[P] - 2:04

44. The Vault (Alternate)[P] - 2:52

45. The Vault (Alternate Performance) - 2:11

46. Message For Holly (Original Version)[O] - 2:52

47. Message For Holly (Revised Version)[O] - 2:58

48. Happy Trails (Tracked Film Edit) - 1:13

49. We've Got Each Other (From the movie Man On Fire; written by John Patrick Scott) - 1:56

50. Resolution and Hyperspace (Excerpt) (From the movie Aliens; James Horner) - 2:47

51. Wild Percussion[P] - 2:16

52. Roy Rogers Meets Beethoven's 9th (Source) - 1:33

53. Winter Wonderland (Source) (written by Felix Bernard and Dick Smith) - 1:26

54. Let It Snow (Source) (Performed by Michael Kamen; Written by Sammy Cahn and Jule Styne) - 1:58

55. Christmas In Hollis (RUN-DMC) - 2:58

Disc 3

56. Main Title (Film Edit) - 0:36

57. Seeing Holly (Film Mix) - 1:05

58. The Phone Goes Dead / Party Crashers (Extended Opening)[O] - 2:22

59. The Nakatomi Plaza (Takagi's Death) (Orchestra Only) - 1:47
60. Wiring The Roof (Film Mix Excerpt) - 0:58
61. Tony Approaches (Film Mix) - 1:44
62. Going After John (Film Mix) - 4:33
63. Al Powell Approaches (Film Mix) - 2:32
64. Al Powell Approaches (Alternate)[P] - 2:37
65. Under The Table (His Bag Is Missing) (Film Edit) - 1:25
66. John Is Found Out (Film Mix) - 5:54
67. Bill Clay Pt. 1 (Film Mix) - 2:08
68. Bill Clay Pt. 2 (Extended)[O] - 2:08
69. Shooting The Glass - 1:08
70. Message For Holly (Original Version) (Orchestra Only)[O] - 2:53
71. The Battle (Alternate Excerpt)[O] - 1:19
72. Wild Take[P] - 1:29
73. Roy Rogers Meets Beethoven's Ninth (Alternate)[P] - 1:36
74. Hip Hop Christmas (Source)[P] - 1:44

[P] – *Previously unreleased*
[O] – *Contains originally unreleased material*

DO YOU REALLY THINK YOU HAVE A CHANCE AGAINST US, MR. COWBOY?

John McClane's injuries

There's no doubt that we love everyman blue-collar worker John McClane and how he rises to the occasion, constantly risking life and limb to save his estranged wife Holly and the more than two dozen other hostages trapped in Nakatomi Plaza. But, putting aside the fantasy elements of the situation, one must wonder how the average person might actually fare when faced with the injuries he sustained in a single night.

In a January 15, 2015, *The Week* feature article by Lauren Hansen entitled "Diagnosing Die Hard's craziest injuries: A professional weighs in," the author explores that. And, after consulting with Dr. Ryan St. Clair of the Palo Alto Medical Foundation, Hansen concludes that John McClane should have been a quadriplegic with bowel and bladder disfunction by the end of the film.

Several other articles and medical professionals have weighed in on the realism of the injuries and the heroic stunts performed in the film, including Dr. Ed Hope, an Emergency Medicine Doctor and Teaching Fellow in the UK in a December 23, 2021, YouTube video called "How many times does DIE HARD die in DIE HARD? // Doctor Reacts." In that video, Hope shares that it's likely McClane would have died 7 times during the course of the film.

Let's explore the various injuries and stunts McClane performs in the movie with a look at the more realistic results in terms of physical, emotional, and psychological trauma as shared by these two medical professionals.

The first scuffle with Tony, the tall blond thug, where he gets tossed about through metal two-by-four drywall studs and then has his head slammed into the wall three times.

While it's unlikely these actions would have broken a rib, Dr. Hope says, McClane would have received multiple bruises and abrasions. It was the head slams, he says, that could easily have caused a concussion or a brain contusion (bruise), possibly even an intercranial bleed, or even an extradural hematoma, where the blood lies on the outside of the brain and starts to compress the brain, which can ultimately be fatal by forcing the brain out of the bottom of the skull (brain herniation)

Rolling down a flight of metal stairs while struggling with Tony.

Dr. Hope describes the fall down stairs as a significant traumatic event that would involve injuries to the skull, spine, and ribs, not to mention internal organ damage (such as pneumothorax—collapsed lung) or limb fractures. Dr. St. Claire says it's not uncommon for people to die while falling down a set of stairs, with the two most common causes of death being subdural hematoma (bleeding between the brain and the skull) and cerebral edema (brain swelling after blunt trauma), John McClane would likely have sustained minimal injuries since he was mostly on top of his foe on the ride down.

Catching himself by his fingertips after falling down two flights when missing the first horizontal ventilation shaft opening.

Considering how unlikely it would be for a sweat-slicked 185-pound man to be able to stop a fall of what appears to be at least twenty feet by only the tips of his fingers, this is almost certain death. Dr. Hope jokes that saving himself in that way is presumably "a brief hallucination as he dies in a mess at the bottom of the elevator shaft."

The explosion from the bottom of the elevator shaft that catches McClane and throws him forward.

"He gets pretty caught up in the flames and has not much protection," says Dr. Hope, "so he could have significant burns to his body." He might also experience some blast injuries, such as primary injuries from air pressure change perforating his ear drum, even secondary blast injuries such as being struck with shrapnel entering his body, or tertiary blast injuries from being thrown and landing awkwardly.

Eating a "1000-year-old" Twinkie.

Though McClane quips in jest to Al Powell at the age of the Twinkie, Dr. Hope jokes that the main side effect from eating a rather stale Twinkie might be loose stool for a couple of days.

Being shot at by Marco when crawling on his back under the boardroom table.

John scrambles on the floor under the boardroom table on his back while Marco, standing on top of the table, shoots at him. As they reach the end of the table, Marco mocks him, saying he should never hesitate when he has a chance to shoot someone. McClane shoots him through the boardroom table with his handgun and quips: "Thanks for the advice."

Marco is equipped with a much more powerful gun and could have easily killed John by shooting him through the table in the way that he himself was shot. One has to wonder at why he didn't do that; unless he was being cocky and wanted to "play" with his prey first.

Running barefoot across a room covered in broken glass.

"McClane's feet would undeniably be badly cut," says Dr. St. Claire, concluding that he would at the very least need proper suturing and oral antibiotics. He goes on to say that the average person might be in so much pain that they wouldn't be able to walk. Dr. Hope says that washing the wounds in the running water of the sink and dressing the woods to prevent additional dirt from getting in would help reduce the chance of infection. But both Dr. St. Claire and Dr. Hope share that there's a risk of smaller pieces of glass or other foreign bodies remaining in the wound undetected that could cause granuloma and cheloid formation. Dr. Hope would also want to make sure he was up to date with his tetanus vaccines to reduce the risk of wound infection.

The numerous punches and kicks thrown and taken in the fight with Karl.

"He would likely have a few broken bones in his hands," says Dr. Hope. "Most likely metacarpal fractures; so, breaking the bone up to the knuckle—often referred to as a boxer's fracture" which can happen when punching something solid such as a bad guy's face.

The powerful kicking he receives from Karl would likely have resulted in broken ribs, but there is also a concern about damage to the lungs. "Added to that, he gets kicked in the face" Dr. Hope continues. "And this could easily kill him from a traumatic brain injury" not to mention facial bone fracture.

Receiving a gunshot wound to the back of the shoulder.

Upon careful reviewing of the scene Dr. St. Claire says it appears that McClane sustains a grazing bullet injury. "If the wound is superficial, does not lacerate an artery, and does not cause significant damage to the deltoid muscle, it is not impossible that McClane could shrug it off and keep fighting." But, he adds, handgun bullets can be extremely hot when fired, so the heat of the bullet could have automatically self-cauterized the wound, reducing the amount of blood loss.

Dr. Hope concurs with the diagnosis of this being a mostly superficial wound, as he notices that McClane is able to move his shoulders when he raises his arms above (and then behind) his head in the final confrontation with Gruber. Anything deeper, he says, could result in fractures of the scapula, the humerus, or the clavicle.

Performing a one hundred foot "bungee jump" with a fire hose.

Ignoring the physics of whether the firehose or the reel it's attached to that gets locked against a ledge on the roof of the building would actually hold a nearly 200-pound man from a fall of that height, there is the shock and trauma from the sudden stop itself to consider.

"Best case scenario, given this force," Dr. Hope says, "he would likely sever his spine, fracturing his spinal cord" which would lead to the paralysis of the legs.

In his analysis, Dr. St. Claire considers mathematical details of the force involved. "Let's assume McClane falls 30 meters (98 feet) before the hose stops him. If McClane weighs 70 kilograms (220 pounds), falls 30 meters, and is stopped by a fire hose made of relatively inelastic material, which extends by only 1.5 meters when stretched, he experiences a force of 14.6 kilonewtons." Dr. St. Claire goes on to share that U.S. Air Force guidelines state the human body can't endure more than 12 kilonewtons without serious injury.

He states that the most likely spinal cord injuries from this type of fall would be fractures of the C5 through C7 vertebrates in the neck. And, assuming that a broken neck wouldn't kill him, that type of injury usually would lead to quadriplegia, bowel, bladder, and sexual dysfunction, and difficulty maintaining proper body temperature, heart rate, and blood pressure.

Crashing through a glass window

While the glass has been weakened from a series of rapid-fire gunshots, McClane would have been injured from the impact with the glass; not to mention the damage from the broken shards of glass likely embedded in his body from that impact and falling on top of the pieces when landing on his back.

That landing is likely to have broken any ribs not already broken from the sudden stop of his plunge off the side of the building and left him winded. And then there's the additional shock and force of when the fire hose reel releases from where it had been hooked, falls, and yanks McClane forward towards the window. That would have further exacerbated the spinal injuries.

Smoking

The biggest killer in *Die Hard*, Dr. Hope says, is smoking. In a single evening McClane smokes six cigarettes, which suggests that he perhaps would smoke between fifteen to twenty cigarettes a day, which would likely be doing more damage to him over his life than any of these bad guys. "So, cigarettes are the real villain in the film," Dr. Hope quips, "and this is probably what will kill him in the end."

JUST THE FAX, MA'AM

Miscellaneous trivia

While this entire book contains behind-the-scenes information and trivia, there were additional bits and pieces of trivial information that were cut from those chapters, didn't seem to work anywhere else, or might be intriguing tidbits derived from those longer pieces.

To that end, I've collected them here. Please be aware that there may be a bit of overlap between this chapter and elements that have already been covered elsewhere in this book.

—

Die Hard finished 1998 as the seventh-highest grossing film of 1988 and was the only action/adventure movie in the top ten. That year's top 10 films sorted by gross sales were:

- *Who Framed Roger Rabbit* ($238.1 million)
- *Rain Man* ($172.8 million)
- *Coming to America* ($128.1 million)
- *Big* ($114.9 million)
- *Twins* ($111.9 million)
- *Crocodile Dundee II* ($109.3 million)
- *Die Hard* ($83 million)
- *The Naked Gun* ($78.7 million)
- *Cocktail* ($78.2 million)
- *Beetlejuice* ($73.7 million)

—

In the original book that *Die Hard* was based on, the bad guys were a politically motivated terrorist group lead by Anton Gruber. Writer Jeb Stuart adapted Anton into Hans and also made them thieves masquerading as terrorists, saying that everybody likes a good caper movie.

—

Another change Stuart made was the company where the Christmas party was being held. In the novel it was the Klaxon Oil corporation but was adapted into the Japanese Nakatomi Trading.

—

One of the first names screenwriter Jeb Stuart came up with for the main character was John Ford, a nod to the legendary director. But Lloyd Levin told him the name was too important in the history of 20th Century Fox to use in an action movie. He then ran through fifty last names before landing on his own Celtric root inspired McClane.

—

The address (2121 Avenue of the Stars, Los Angeles, CA 90067) and phone numbers (213-203-3723) that appear on the screen of the 911 dispatcher are/were the real-life address for Fox Plaza which became Nakatomi Plaza in the movie.

—

Some of the movie's most memorable scenes were created on the fly. Script writing veteran Steven de Souza hastily wrote several scenes based on inspiration taking place on the set itself and would even phone in at various times during the shoot to suggest additional ad hoc lines. The entire sequence in which Hans Gruber pretends to be a hostage when he runs into John McClane up on the roof, was inspired from De Souza overhearing actor Alan Rickman demonstrating his American accent to the film crew. Galvanized by this, De Souza hammered out a fresh page of script, and the scene was incorporated into the movie.

—

John McTiernan turned down producer Joel Silver's offer to direct *Die Hard* at least three times, claiming he didn't want to do a terrorist movie. They simply weren't fun the way a "robbery" movie was.

—

Die Hard was Alan Rickman's first Hollywood movie. And prior to accepting it he had private doubts about taking the role of Hans Gruber, which he shared in an April 2015 BAFTA article entitled 'Alan Rickman: A Life in Pictures.' After reading the script he said "What the hell is this? I'm not doing an action movie." But agents and friends explained how rare it was to be in Hollywood for only two days and getting offered such an opportunity.

—

The original logo for the Nakatomi corporation looked too much like a swastika. The one they ended up using was inspired by a Samurai helmet clan seal that producer Joel Silver had discovered when browsing an auction catalog.

—

The price of the 1979 hardcover novel *Nothing Lasts Forever* was $9.95 USD. The ISBN (International Standard Book Number) was 0-393-01249-2.

—

The "inspiration" for how he could adapt the novel *Nothing Lasts Forever* into a screenplay came the night Jeb Stuart got into a fight with his wife and then left in his car. As he was trying to figure out how to apologize to her—because he realized she had been right—he drove into a refrigerator box that had fallen on the highway in front of him. The box, fortunately, was empty, but that's when he realized what the movie would be about.

"It's not about a sixty-year-old man who drops his forty-year-old daughter off a building," Jeb says in the Season 1, epi-sode of 4 of *The Movies That Made Us*. "It's about a thirty-year-old guy who should have said he's sorry to his wife 'cause bad stuff happens."

—

Before the role of John McClane was of-fered to Bruce Willis, it had been offered to actors such as Clint Eastwood, Sylvest-er Stallone; Arnold Schwarzenegger, Richard Gere, Burt Reynolds, and James Caan.

—

Even Bruce Willis had to initially turn the movie down because of his commitment to the television show *Moonlighting*. If it wasn't for his co-star Cybill Shepherd get-ting pregnant, forcing the show's record-ing to shut down for six weeks, Willis would not have been able to take the part.

—

Actor Bruce Willis's first night of filming, in November 1987 was a most harrowing experience, and a far cry from the witty banter and snippy one-liners Willis exchanged with actress Cybill Shepherd on the set of *Moonlighting*. Willis described standing on the edge of the top of a five-story parking garage having a firehose strapped to him and being slathered with something. When he asked what they were covering him with he was told it was so he didn't catch fire when they blew up huge bags of gasoline behind him when he jumped.

"When I jumped," Willis told *Entertainment Weekly*, "the force of the explosion blew me out to the very edge of the air bag I was supposed to land on."

When Willis landed, the crew came running over, and he expected them to be applauding him for a great stunt. Instead, they were checking to see if he was still alive, because they thought he'd missed the bag.

Incredulous he asked: "Why would you shoot this scene first?"

He was told that if he were killed closer to the end of the movie it would cost them a lot more money to reshoot the whole thing with another actor.

—

Karl, the bad guy who survived right up until the bitter end in the movie—and the toughest thug John McClane fights—was played by a man who was initially a ballet dancer. Alexander Godunov began dancing at the age of nine in the same classes as Mikhail Baryshnikov before later defecting from Russia to the United States and eventually beginning a career as an actor.

—

Playing movie characters inspired by Roderick Thorp's Joe Leland in *The Detective* (Sinatra) and *Nothing Lasts Forever* (Willis) is not the only thing that Frank Sinatra and Bruce Willis have in common.

Willis's very first big screen appearance and Frank Sinatra's last starring role also coincided.

Bruce Willis was an un-credited extra in the 1980 movie *The First Deadly Sin*. In a scene where Sintra, playing Sergeant Edward Delaney, is walking out the door of a restaurant, he passes Bruce Willis, whose face is mostly obscured by a hat worn low and covering his eyes as he walks in.

—

The scene where John McClane falls down the elevator shaft and misses the first vent opening was not in the script. When filming, the stunt man missed on the first take, so film editor Frank J. Urioste incorporated that miss in order to notch up the thrill of that fall.

—

The letters on the side of the ambulance that Theo drives is misspelled as "LOS ANGELES CITY FIRE DEPARMENT" (the t is missing in *department*). The crew didn't notice this until after filming was completed.

—

A heavily stained and blood-soaked white vest style t-shirt that John McClane wore throughout *Die Hard* is at the National Museum of American History at the Smithsonian Institution. Actor Bruce Willis donated it in June 2007 along with a movie poster, a prop police badge, and a script from the 2007 sequel *Live Free or Die Hard*.

The items initially went on display in July 2007 as part of the "Treasures of American History" exhibit, hosted by the Air and Space Museum. Also included in the exhibition were the boxing gloves from *Rocky* and the ruby slippers from *The Wizard of Oz*.

The shirt donated by Willis was one of 34 shirts wore by the actor and the stuntmen who worked on the film.

In a 2020 exploration entitled "Every Stain a Story: The many dirty undershirts of John McClane in *Die Hard*" textile artist and researcher Urs A. Georg Dierker said: "The *Die Hard* undershirts are a fascinating example of how an item of fashion, in this case everyday men's underwear, is adapted for film costume and embedded with a variety of meanings before, during and after filming."

—

Nakatomi Plaza is—in reality—the headquarters of 20th Century Fox, the studio that made *Die Hard*. The building was also under construction at the time, which more easily leant itself to several key scenes in the movie.

—

The costume department had seventeen different t-shirts in various stages of "degradation" that Bruce Willis wore for different moments in the movie's timeline. (There were thirty-four in total worn by Willis and various stuntmen).

—

Production designer Jackson De Govia said in a *Die Hard* DVD extra audio commentary that the room where the hostages are held was supposed to be Frank Lloyd Wright's Fallingwater, purchased, disassembled, then re-assembled in Nakatomi headquarters like a trophy.

—

A few of the potential movie titles that had allegedly been kicked around for the 6th film in the franchise are *Die Hardest*, *Cross My Heart and Hope to Die Hard,* and *Die Hard 6 Feet Under*.

—

The original script of *Die Hard* took place over a three-day period, but John McTiernan was inspired by William Shakespeare's *A Midsummer Night's Dream* and had the vision that it, like the play, should take place in a single night.

—

The scene where John McClane and Hans Gruber meet at the top of the building was inspired by script writer Steven de Souza overhearing actor Alan Rickman doing a fake American accent for cast and crew members during a break in filming.

—

The infamous line "Yippee-Ki-Yay Moth-erfucker" was actually written as "Yipee-yi-yea" in the second revised draft (Oct 2, 1987).

—

Actor De'voreaux White (Argyle) says that everyone pronounces his name "Deh-voh-row" but that it's supposed to be pronounced "Deh-voy-yay" and that he thinks his parents were "smoking pot or something."

—

McClane jumping off the roof of Nakatomi tower with a fire hose wrapped around his waist was a bit of a nod to actor/stunt man Howard Clayton Lloyd Sr. who performed a similar stunt in the 1923 short film *Safety Last*.

—

The fear that you see on Hans Gruber's face when he falls off Nakatomi tower is real. Actor Alan Rickman performed the stunt himself and was held about forty feet above an airbag for it. Stuntman and stunt coordinator Charlie Picerni told Rickman he would be released in the pattern of "3 . . . 2 . . . 1 . . . Go!" but privately instructed the rig operator to let him go on "1."

And, in case he was injured in the fall, as Rickman said in an interview, they were very careful to make it his very last shot as Gruber in the film.

—

The fake ambulance that the bad guys were supposed to escape from the aftermath of the top of the building exploding wasn't a part of the original script. It was a last-minute addition to the script from writer Steven de Souza who needed to invent a way they could plan their getaway. So, he used that same device which he'd written into an episode of the television series *Spirit*.

—

When the trailer was first released to theatres, the minute Bruce Willis's face appeared, the audience laughed. In some cases, the audiences resoundingly booed. This led the studio to taking Willis's face off the marketing posters for the film about a month before it was to debut. His face wasn't returned to the posters until a few weeks after the movie's release.

—

Reginald VelJohnson (Al Powell) was living in his mother's basement when he got the call to audition for the film. At the time he was broke, had only had a few small television and movie roles, and was considering giving up on his acting career.

—

VelJohnson is best known for playing police characters. Not only did he play Al Powell in *Die Hard* and *Die Hard 2*, but he also played a cop in *Turner & Hooch* (1989) and was cast as Carlton "Carl" Otis Winslow in the *Perfect Strangers* episode "Crimebusters" and reprised the role, later that same year (1989) in the spin-off show *Family Matters*.

—

The actor who attends to Al Powell's head injury from his police cruiser crash was played by actor Anthony Peck, and was credited as Young Cop. Peck also played Detective Ricky Walsh in *Die Hard with a Vengeance*.

—

The logo on the transport truck the bad guys drive into the parking garage of Nakatomi Plaza contains an "in joke." Production designer Jackson De Govia said that Pacific Courier translates to either "bringer of peace" or "messenger of peace." De Govia used the same logo and company name in the movie *Speed* (where it appears on the side of an airplane). He used it again in *Die Hard: With A Vengeance* which features Hans Gruber's brother as the villain. In that third *Die Hard* movie the truck (which is blown into the air) has the words "Atlantic Courier" on it. It is presumed—through De Govia's inside joke—that it is a subsidiary of the same company.

—

The opening scene on the plane was actually filmed on an airplane that was being towed around in circles on a runway for the shoot.

—

A painted backing was designed to create the Los Angeles backdrop seen from the office building shots in the late afternoon, evening, and night. Wrapping around the 34th floor set, it was 380 feet long and incorporated backlighting and included animated lights to create day and night effects. It is supposedly still a part of Fox's

ongoing inventory and is said to be occa-
sionally used for other 20th Century Fox
films.

—

Among many of the improvised lines in
the film by Bruce Willis were when he
says "Hi, Honey" as he arrives for the final confrontation with Hans Gruber.

—

Al Leong, who played Uli, the Asian
henchman in Hans' crew, had very few
lines in the movie because he was pri-
marily a stuntman, not an actor. And the
moment where he steals the candy bar
from the front lobby concession stand is
an ad hoc bit Leong asked director John
McTiernan if it was okay for his character
to do.

—

When explaining the situation to Powell
on the radio, McClane tells him that the
bad guys have "missiles, automatic weapons, and enough plastic explosives to orbit Arnold Schwarzenegger." Arnie was
originally considered for the role of

McClane. So was Sylvester Stallone. The three worked together in *The Expendables* (2010) and *The Expendables 2* (2012).

—

The dispatch supervisor—who some say looks a little like Willis's wife at the time Demi Moore—was played by Diana James. James also appears as a stewardess aboard Holly's flight in *Die Hard 2*.

—

The phrase "Die Hard" doesn't translate well into other language. So, in some other countries, the movie had to be retitled.

- French: *The Crystal Trap*
- German: *Die Slowly*
- Greek: *Very Hard to Die*
- Norwegian: *Action Skyscraper*
- Polish: *The Glass Trap*
- Romain: *Difficult to Kill*
- Spanish: *The Crystal Jungle* or *Very Hard to Die*

—

De'voreaux White (Argyle) actually punched Clarence Gilyard Jr. (Theo) through the driver window after the limo driver crashed his car into the side of the ambulance. The moment where he is shaking his hand is White expressing actual pain from the punch. In previous takes, White was told the punch didn't look real enough, and there was a bit of conflict over the scene. Those elements led to the punch accidentally becoming a real one.

—

Theo is one of only two of the bad guys who survives to the end of the film. (Which worked out nicely in bringing him back for the 2020 *DieHard* battery commercial. He ends up being "toast" at the end of that one). The other thug to survive is Kristoff (played by Gérard Bonn) who operated as Theo's assistant. Kristoff is cold cocked by the rifle butt of McClane's gun as he rounds the corner at the top of the ramp. He falls to the ground and the bearer bonds he was holding fan out across the floor.

—

The use of the pin-up girl poster at the top of the elevator shaft that McClane addresses one of the times he passes them demonstrates him using them as a "geographic marker" as he moved about the building. It's in line with the scene showing him writing down the names of the bad guys on his arm and when he mutters the details of what he has noticed is happening on each floor when he first escapes into the stairwell.

—

The centerfold at the top of the elevator shaft is of November 1987 *Playboy* Playmate Pamelia Stein. Two other *Playboy* Playmates have bit parts in the movie. The first is July 1988 Playmate Terri Lynn Doss, who plays the woman at the airport dressed in white who rushes past McClane to jump into the arms of another passenger in a green shirt. And one of the female hostages at the Christmas party seen sparingly was played by May 1982 *Playboy* Playmate Kym Malin.

—

Despite appearing topless in other films, *Playboy* Playmate Kym Malin was not the half-naked partygoer caught having sex with a fellow employee in one of the offices—distracting them enough to allow McClane to exit through the fire escape. That role was played by actress Cheryl Baker.

—

The scene in Ellis's office where John and Holly argue was written when script writer Steven E. de Souza had the two actors improvise for about an hour and a half. He took the best pieces of what they improvised and laid them back on top of the script, claiming it was one of the most "collegial" projects he's worked on.

—

Two references to the Japanese naval attack on Pearl Harbor on December 7, 1941, occur in the film. The first occurs when—after McClane questions whether the Japanese celebrate Christmas—Takagi explains that they're flexible. And that "Pearl Harbor didn't work out, so we got you with tape decks." The second time is when Theo breaks the code key for the vault with the password "Akagi" (Red Castle, in English). It's the name of one of the Japanese aircraft carriers which carried out the strike on Pearl Harbor.

James Shigeta who played Mr. Takagi also played Vice Admiral Chiūichi Nagumo, one of the architects of the attack on Pearl Harbor in the film *The Battle of Midway* (1976).

—

Actor Reginald VelJohnson said that after his appearances in the first two *Die Hard* movies, he was frequently teased by both friends and strangers for his character's obsession with Twinkies.

—

The firearms used in the film are—as in most action films—real firearms modified to function with blanks. Director John McTiernan wanted vivid, "exaggerated realism" in the muzzle flashes. Weapons specialist Michael Papac specially modified the firearms involved to be much louder and involve more dramatic flashes.

—

In a 2019 interview Bruce Willis shared that due to an incident in the first *Die Hard* film, he suffers from two-third partial hearing loss in his left ear. It happened during the scene where McClane kills the terrorist standing on top of the table whose last words are: "Next time you have a chance to kill someone, don't hesitate." McClane, lying on the floor says, "Thanks for the advice!" and fires through the conference table. Willis suffered severe damage to his left ear due to the close quarters and closed space under the table and nearby Plexiglas used to protect the actor from flying shell casings and wood splinters.

—

In an interview released for the 30th anniversary of the movie, Bonnie Bedelia stated that Alan Rickman is the first thing she thinks of when someone mentions *Die Hard*. The two became friends during the filming and regularly had lunch together while shooting the movie.

—

Bruce Willis received $5 million for his role as John McClane. At the time this was an unprecedented amount and it had to be approved by Fox President Rupert Murdoch.

—

Clint Eastwood owned the film rights to Roderick Thorp's novel *Nothing Lasts Forever* in the early 1980s and had intended to produce and star in its film adaptation. But nothing came of it, and he let the option lapse.

—

The line "Hans . . . Bubby!" was an ad-lib by actor Hart Boucher (Ellis).

—

Bruce Willis wore specially made "rubber shoes" designed to look like his own feet. These were used in various scenes to protect his feet from the broken glass on the floor and other hazards encountered in the scenes where McClane is rushing about. In a few scenes if you look closely, you can see these "unnaturally large" feet in use.

—

9 of the 12 bad guys in the movie were over six feet tall. Only a couple of them were actually German. They were cast due to their "menacing" appearances rather than their nationality.

—

While McClane is in the restroom dealing with the damage to his bleeding feet, he quips the following line to Al Powell. "All things being equal, I'd rather be in Philadelphia." This is a reference to an old joke from W.C. Fields that was shared in *Vanity Fair* magazine in 1925. He proposed that his tombstone should read: "Here lies W.C. Fields. I would rather be living in Philadelphia." Fields grew up and got his start in Philadelphia. Variations of this line have been used by others over the years, notably President Ronald Regan referencing it when in hospital after his assassination attempt in 1981.

—

When Hans Gruber mocks John McClane by saying this tale wouldn't end like an American Western, "Grace Kelly riding off into the sunset with John Wayne," McClane corrects him by saying it was Gary Cooper. The film they are referencing is 1952's *High Noon.* In that film, Cooper, as the town Marshall, must face a gang of killers alone. Nice meta reference.

—

Bruce Willis did a number of his own stunts in the film, including riding on the top of the elevator. Filming that allegedly "scared the shit" out of Director John McTiernan.

—

Though *Die Hard* is an action movie, no real "action" happens until about 18 minutes into the film, when Karl and Theo enter the lobby and Karl shoots the security guard.

—

Al Powell is singing the Christmas song "Let it Snow" as the body McClane tossed out the window descends toward his car.

—

Die Hard is one of those rare action films where the hero and the main villain don't get into a fist fight. This further illustrates that the conflict is a battle of wits between the two.

—

When Ellis is "negotiating" with Hans Gruber Karl pours Coca-Cola® into a glass for him. This is possibly a humorous subtle reference to Ellis, previously seen snorting cocaine, having asked if they had any coke, which they mistook for the soda.

—

Al Powell tells Deputy Chief Dwayne Robinson that he believes the man on the radio he was talking to is a cop because he mentioned being able to spot a phony ID. Robinson responds that he "could be a fucking bartender for all we know." Prior to becoming a well-known actor, Willis was a bartender.

—

As McClane watches Al Powell circle the Nakatomi parking lot he quips: "Who's driving this car, Stevie Wonder?" The song "Skeletons" by Stevie Wonder in playing on the limousine stereo in the background while Argyle is on the phone down in the parking garage.

—

Die Hard is the longest movie in the franchise, clocking in at 132 minutes. The length of the others, in descending order, are *Live Free and Die Hard* (129 minutes), *Die Hand with a Vengeance* (128 minutes), *Die Hard 2* (124 minutes), and *A Good Day to Die Hard* (97 minutes).

—

The album soundtrack for *Die Hard* was not released until almost 14 full years after the movie, in February 2002. It was reissued in November and March of 2017, and then remastered in November 2018 for the 30th anniversary of the film's release.

—

This being his first action film, Alan Rickman was completely unfamiliar with and uncomfortable with guns. He had to be trained by casting director Jackie Burch on how to hold a weapon. Without the training, he would hold the gun in a limp manner. And he would constantly flinch whenever he pulled the trigger, which is why, whenever Gruber fires a gun, it quickly cuts away from him. But if you look closely at the scene where he shoots Takagi, you can catch the wince.

—

The "real" die-hard of the film is most likely Karl. In a *Dr Hopes Sick Notes* YouTube video Dr. Ed Hope shares that no "one ever talks about Karl." He has to deal with the emotional hit of his brother dying, receives at least a dozen punches, takes a heavy beating to the head, is hanged, survives the rooftop explosion, and receives five gunshots to the chest before he dies.

JUST A FLY IN THE OINTMENT, HANS

Bloopers, mistakes, errors, omissions, & goofs

As much as we love a film, and as close as *Die Hard* is to the perfect modern classic action film, there are still a few errors that always make their way into the final cut. It's not all that different than the fact that virtually every single book published has at least a handful of typographical errors.

And so, even though we adore this movie, we can still acknowledge a few of the errors that made it into *Die Hard*.

• When Joseph Takagi steps out of his office to congratulate the staff on their recent business deal and to wish them a Merry Christmas and Happy New Year, there is a small orchestra playing on the balcony. They are seen again when John McClane first arrives on the 30th floor.

But, as the hostages are all rounded up, the orchestra members seem to have dis-appeared.

• The song that the orchestra is playing (Bach's *Brandenburg Concerto 3 in G Major, BWV 1048 - Allegro moderato*) as Takagi addresses the troops and McClane is ar-riving at the airport is still playing when—what has to be at least twenty minutes later—John arrives at the Christmas party. The piece is only about six minutes and twenty-five seconds long. So, unless the orchestra doesn't have many songs in its repertoire and is repeating their play-list, this is a continui-ty gaff.

• In the first establishing shot of John and Argyle in the limousine the oversized teddy can be seen in the middle of the back seat. But in the shot showing the view of the back via the rearview mirror, the bear seems to be situated significantly closer to the one side.

• As John McClane is looking for his wife's name on the computer directory, her last name is properly spelled GEN-NARO. But once he taps the button, the spelling changes to GENNERO. That is also the incorrect way the name is spelled on the door of her office. Holly Gennaro's name is represented inconsistently throughout the film. In the book the movie was based on, the last name was spelled Gennaro. In the script the name is inconsistently spelled both Gennaro and Gennero, with 10 instances using the "e" and two using the "a." However, in the film credits the character is identified as *Holly Gennaro McClane*.

• When Hans and his crew first arrive at the basement of the Nakatomi building and all exit the back of the transport truck you can clearly see that it's empty. But near the end of the movie Theo drives an ambulance out of the truck. (*This error has been acknowledged by the filmmakers*).

• As Hans is leading the bad guys from the truck through the basement, the one on his right (the one who looks like Huey Lewis who takes the spot of the lobby security guard) appears to be on a direct collision course for the doorway wall just as it cuts over to Theo hacking into the computer system.

• Takagi tells Gruber, when he is asking for his password that any information he could possibly get would be changed when "they wake up in Tokyo in the morning." But it has to already be 10 AM or later in Tokyo at that point. Though the time of day isn't stated, it's already after sunset, which, in late December in Los Angeles, would be around 4:50 PM. And PST (Pacific Standard time) to JST (Japan Standard Time) is 17 hours.

• When John sets off the fire alarm, Hans tells one of his crew to call the fire department and report it as a false alarm. The fire trucks are seen turning around, apparently being called off, without ever reaching the building. Standard procedures for many fire departments is to independently verify for themselves that there is no fire, by arriving at the scene and making an assessment.

• Shortly after the bad guys first launch their assault, when John ascends to one of the floors under construction, he looks out a window and sees a woman in a window across the street. The view makes it appear as if the building is close, but in all other shots of Nakatomi tower, there doesn't appear to be any other buildings that close.

• In the split-second before Hans shoves aside the head of Tony, the bad guy with the message "NOW I HAVE A MA-CHINE GUN HO-HO-HO" on it, you can see the actor playing Tony moves his head slightly.

• As Sergeant Al Powell is muttering the lyrics to "Let it Snow" while getting back into his car after quickly checking the lobby at Nakatomi Plaza, he sings "but nobody has no place to go" instead of "and since we've no place to go."

• The gash on Al Powell's head that he received when his car crashed seems to have disappeared by the time that Depu-ty Police Chief Dwayne Robinson arrives.

• John McClane's white t-shirt turns dark green after he crawls through the series of ventilation shafts. The shirt would most definitely have been stained by the grime and dirt from the ducts, particularly since there'd be a lot of particles present from the construction, but the shirt is almost uniformly stained, rather than smudged only where the shirt would have come in contact with the grimy surfaces.

• The bad guys fire a rocket launcher at the LAPD's armored car twice. And BOTH times they fire, the exact same window explodes. It should only have done that the first time they shot through it.

• In the sequence where the FBI sends two helicopters to surprise the "terrorists" with there are several shots of a pair of helicopters on their approach to the building. But after about the 1 hour 54-minute mark in the movie, you only ever see a single helicopter. The second one seems to have disappeared.

- Ignoring the physics of the spine-breaking "bungee jump" with the fire-hose, there's no way that McClane's fall would have been broken. As the metal reel of the firehose disengaged from its mount, it catches on the inside vertical rise of the rooftop ledge. If you look closely, you'll see there's not much to "hold" it in place from a nearly 200-pound man falling about 100 feet. Perhaps if the top of the metal reel had been caught *under* the visible ledge on that vertical rise, instead of against it, it would have held long enough for McClane to smash his way through the window the way he does.

CONCLUSION

As I mentioned in the introduction, I can't tell you exactly the first time I watched *Die Hard*. It came out the summer I had graduated from high school, and I remember it being a pretty intense and busy summer for me. So it's entirely possible I didn't catch it until a year or so later when it was released on VHS.

But when I did see it, I knew it was a movie I would watch again and again.

And I've purchased numerous copies of the movie on VHS, DVD and Blu-ray over the years. As I write this, in addition to the stand-alone films in both formats there are at least two different DVD and Blu-ray box sets of the movie in our house.

You know, for the extra features.

Because it's not enough for me to re-watch a beloved film. I find it fun to explore and learn as much as I can about behind the scenes.

Once my son—who turns 19 around the time of the 35th Anniversary of the movie's release—was old enough, we watched *Die*

Hard together. And the two of us have enjoyed watching the film repeatedly together over the years. We often follow it up with a viewing of *Die Hard 2*, particularly if we're doing our viewing during the holidays. But we have enjoyed all the films in the franchise together, hanging on the edge of our seats during the thrills, and laughing at the quips and humorous moments.

There are only a handful of movies I've seen as many times as I've seen *Die Hard*, and few thrillers are on that very short list.

Why do I, and millions of others around the world keep returning to it? Is it the reluctant hero flawed everyman John McClane who wise-cracks his way through the tightest of spots, demonstrating Bruce Willis's nuanced skill in owning that role? Is it the ingeniously unforgettable pompous yet charming bad guy performed brilliantly by Alan Rickman? Is it Bonne Bedelia's portrayal of the fiercely strong, independent, and fearless leader Holly Genero? Could it be the bro love between McClane and Powell? Or perhaps the snarky commentary of brilliant computer hacker Theo? Maybe it's the bravery of the young Argyle who goes well above and beyond on his first day on the new job?

Perhaps it's all of these, and more.

The writers, the director, the actors, the producers, and everyone involved in bringing together the story that continues to take us on a 132-minute humorous thrill-ride annually have created something truly remarkable in his film.

They not only re-created what an action movie could be, but they heralded in a bold new era in entertainment and filmmaking. Look at the numerous films that have come out ever since that have been described as "Die Hard on a . . ." or "Die Hard in a . . ."

Millions of us have already enjoyed *Die Hard* countless times in the 35 years since the movie's theatrical release. And I'm certain that in another 35 years people will *still* be talking about this movie; not just debating its merits as a Christmas film but talking about what it is that *they* so love about the film and why, like us, they feel compelled to watch it again and again, and again.

That love, that enthusiasm, that passion, will, like the film franchise's main character, be something that dies hard.

Yippee-Ki-Yay, fellow Die Hard fan!

SOURCES & REFERENCES

And further reading

Here is a list of many of the resources used for gathering content and information compiled into this book. They were invaluable in my research.

For further reading, viewing, or listening pleasure, I encourage you to check them out.

Books

- Horner, Doogie & Harrison, JJ (Illus). *A Die Hard Christmas*. San Rafael: Insight Editions, 2017.

- Mottram, James and Cohen, Davis S. *Die Hard: The Ultimate Visual History.* San Rafael: Insight Editions, 2018.

- Taylor-Foster, Kim. *Why We Love Die Hard*. Philadelphia: Running Press, 2022.

- Thorp, Roderick. *Nothing Lasts Forever*. New York: W.W. Norton & Company. 1979.

- Wager, Walter, *58 Minutes*. New York: A TOR Book: New York, 1987.

Videos

- "How many times does DIE HARD die in DIE HARD? // Doctor Reacts." YouTube, Dr Hope's Sick Notes, Dec 23, 2021, https://www.youtube.com/watch?v=OuQTJy_f6PU

- "Yippee Ki Yay by Richard Marsh - Official tour trailer." YouTube, Seabright Productions, Oct 18, 2022, https://www.youtube.com/watch?v=hsMwqbMhkG8

- *The Movies that Made Us.* "Die Hard" (Season 1, Episode 4). Directed by Brian Volk-Weiss. Narrated by Donald Ian Black. The Nacelle Company. Nov 29, 2019.

Articles

- Adrian, Jack, "Obituaries: Roderick Thorp." *Independent*, May 21, 1999.

- Alexander, Julia, "Report: Die Hard 6 is happening and it's going to be a prequel." *Polygon*, Oct 15, 2015.

- "Alan Rickman: A Life in Pictures," BAFTA, April 15, 2015.

- Alter, Ethan, "Is 'Die Hard' a Christmas movie? Cinematographer Jan de Bont says it's 'far-fetched.'" *Yahoo*, Dec 16, 2022.

- Collins, K. Austin. "Die Hard Is as Brilliantly Engineered as a Machine Gun, Even 30 Years Later." *Vanity Fair*, July 13, 2018.

- Crawford, Amy. "Die Hard Donation: Bruce Willis gives John McClane's blood-smeared undershirt to the Smithsonian. Yippee-ki-yay..." *Smithsonian Magazine*, June 30, 2007.

- Dierker, Urs A. Georg (2019), 'Every stain a story: The many dirty undershirts of John McClane in *Die Hard*', *Studies in Costume & Performance*, 4:2, pp. 193–205. January 2020.

- Dhruv Bose, Swaptil. "Settling the debate, why 'Die Hard' is undoubtedly a Christmas movie." Dec 25, 2020.

- Horton, Alex. "Is 'Die Hard' a Christmas movie? Bruce Willis finally has an answer." *The Washington Post*, Jul 16, 2018.

- Kehr, Dave. "Sleek 'Die Hard' Tools Action Film to Perfection." *Chicago Tribune*, July 15, 1988.

- Klassen, Anna, "Steven E. de Souza: Die Hard IS a Christmas Movie." *Final Draft Blog*, July 19, 2018.

- Marsh, Steve. "10 Die Hard Tidbits We Learned From Its Biggest Scene-Stealers." *Vulture*, July 16, 2013.

- The Midnight Rider, "The 25th Anniversary of 'Die Hard' – How John McClane Changed Action Movies (And Us) Forever." *ScreenCrush*, July 15, 2013.

- Nashawaty, Chris, "Bruce Willis: 'If I hadn't done "Die Hard," I'd rip it off'." *Entertainment Weekly*, June 14, 2007.

- Patches, Matt, "The Die Hard prequel McClane died hard because of Disney." *Polygon*, Jul 27, 2021.

- Patches, Matt, "Writer Behind 'Die Hard 6' a.k.a. 'Die Hardest' Explains How the Project Came to Be." *Hollywood.com*, Apr 30, 2013.

- Potter Jordan. "Bruce Willis ends the 'Die Hard' debate: "It's not a Christmas movie"." *Far Out*, Dec 22, 2022.

- Power, Ed, "Die Hard At 30: How The Every-dude Action Movie Defied Expectations And Turned Bruce Willis Into A Star." *The Independent*, November 26, 2018.

- Thomas, Kevin. "'Die Hard' a Slick Flick for Bruce Willis." *LA Times*, July 15, 1988.

- Thurber, John, "Roderick Thorp; Writer of 'Die Hard,' 'The Detective'." *Los Angeles Times*, May 2, 1999.

- Tung, Angela. "A brief history of yippee-ki-yay." *The Week*, Jan 8, 2015.

Misc. Online Resources

- "DieHard legacy." *Advance Auto Parts DieHard*. https://www.diehard.com/legacy/

- "Die Hard." IMDb. https://www.imdb.com/title/tt0095016/

- "Die Hard [Original Motion Picture Soundtrack]." *AllMusic*. ALLMUSIC, NETAKTION LLC. https://www.allmusic.com/album/die-hard-original-motion-picture-soundtrack--mw0000977518/releases

- "Die Hard." *Wikipedia*. https://en.wikipedia.org/wiki/Die_Hard

- "Die Hard (film series)." *Wikipedia*. https://en.wikipedia.org/wiki/Die_Hard_(film_series)

- "Die hard (phrase)." *Wikipedia.* https://en.wikipedia.org/wiki/Die_hard_(phrase)

- "Die Hard (screenplay)." *IMSDb – The Internet Movie Script Database.* https://imsdb.com/scripts/Die-Hard.html

- "Die Hard shirt." – *Smithsonian National Museum of American History.* https://americanhistory.si.edu/collections/search/object/nmah_1324920

- "Die Hard (soundtrack)." *Wikipedia.* https://en.wikipedia.org/wiki/Die_Hard_(soundtrack)

- "Die Hard Wiki." – *Fandom, Inc.* https://diehard.fandom.com/wiki/

- "Roderick Thorp." *Goodreads.* https://www.goodreads.com/author/show/242280.Roderick_Thorp

- "Roderick Thorp." *Wikipedia.* https://en.wikipedia.org/wiki/Roderick_Thorp

- "Yippee Ki Yay (Live)" *Seabright Productions.* https://ykylive.com/

- "Yippee Ki Yay Merry Christmas! A Die Hard Musical Parody." YippeeTheMusical! Yippee Productions LLC. https://www.yippeethemusical.com/

ABOUT THE AUTHOR

Mark's thirty years of experience working in the book industry started in 1992, the same year his first short story appeared in print. He has since published more than thirty books and continues to work as an industry representative and consultant.

When he is not quoting lines from *Die Hard*, Monty Python, John Hughes movies or random song lyrics Mark can be found haunting local bookstores, libraries, and craft beer establishments.

You can find him online at www.markleslie.ca.

SELECTED BOOKS

Movie Trivia

*The Canadian Mounted: A Trivia Guide to
Planes, Trains and Automobiles*

Non-Fiction ("Ghost Stories")

*Haunted Hospitals
Creepy Capital
Tomes of Terror
Spooky Sudbury
Haunted Hamilton*

Fiction

The Canadian Werewolf Series
*A Canadian Werewolf in New York
Stowe Away
Fear and Longing in Los Angeles
Fright Nights, Big City
Lover's Moon
Hex and the City
Only Monsters in the Building*

YOU MIGHT ALSO LIKE

The Canadian Mounted: A Trivia Guide to Planes, Trains and Automobiles

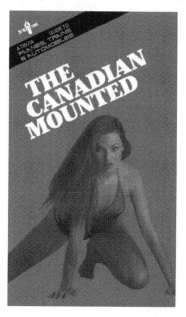

In the movie *Planes, Trains and Automobiles*, John Candy is seen holding a paperback that, in the original script written by John Hughes, reads that Del Griffith is reading a pornographic novel. That is what inspired this trivia book about the film.